I0792993

The TROY STRAWBERRY FESTIVAL

The TROY STRAWBERRY FESTIVAL

A History

David Fong

Foreword by Michael L. Beamish

The History PRESS

Published by The History Press
Charleston, SC
www.historypress.com

Copyright © 2021 by David Fong
All rights reserved

Front cover, clockwise from top left: courtesy of the *Dayton Daily News*, photographer Lisa Powell; courtesy of the *Troy Daily News*, photographer Anthony Weber; courtesy of the *Troy Daily News*, photographer Anthony Weber; courtesy of the *Troy Daily News*, photographer Mike Ullery; courtesy of the *Dayton Daily News*; courtesy of the *Troy Daily News*, photographer Anthony Weber.
Back cover: courtesy of the *Troy Daily News*, photographer Anthony Weber

First published 2021

Manufactured in the United States

ISBN 9781467147125

Library of Congress Control Number: 2020951864

Notice: The information in this book is true and complete to the best of our knowledge. It is offered without guarantee on the part of the author or The History Press. The author and The History Press disclaim all liability in connection with the use of this book.

All rights reserved. No part of this book may be reproduced or transmitted in any form whatsoever without prior written permission from the publisher except in the case of brief quotations embodied in critical articles and reviews.

To Mom and Dad, whom I miss.

CONTENTS

FOREWORD

I am honored to have been asked to write the foreword for David Fong's newest book.

David moved to Troy in 1974 when his father accepted a job at the Troy Friendly's Ice Cream facility and moved his family to our fair city. When the Troy Strawberry Festival began later in the 1970s, Friendly's was here as a major sponsor and a major creator of huge strawberry sundaes. It also sponsored the Friendly's Super Cities Competition, one of the more popular events, the winner of which received a new instrument for their high school band.

I have been associated with the Troy Strawberry Festival in some capacity since 1980. During the 1980s and 1990s, I was part of a winning Friendly's Super Cities team and a winning bed-racing team. I also chaired a variety of festival committees and was fortunate enough to chair the whole festival in 1988. Most recently, I chaired the Golden Couple event that featured a Not-So-Newlywed format for our couples married for more than fifty years. It has been my honor to serve this great festival in so many ways.

The Troy Strawberry Festival attracts hundreds of thousands of individuals and families to our city every year. During the first weekend of June, the Troy downtown and levee come alive. Many nonprofits within our community garner the majority of their annual operating funds from the proceeds of their TSF food booths.

My connection with the author of *The Troy Strawberry Festival* goes way back. We both share a love for our community and especially for our local sports teams. David Fong is an award-winning journalist; I read his sports columns religiously, agreeing with him most of the time. In recent years, he has also authored many human-interest stories, which revealed another facet of his emotional side. He and his wife, Michelle, have two lovely children, Sophie and Max. David can be described as the consummate community supporter and cheerleader. He is a rabid sports enthusiast with an unending love for his Ohio State Buckeyes and his hometown Troy Trojans.

In addition to covering sports in his previous role with the *Troy Daily News*, he has been active in the Troy Strawberry Festival, most notably as a bed race winner himself. After reporting from the festival for many years, he knows its ins and outs, its best activities and, of course, its best strawberry food booths.

He is extremely proud of his hometown and has always felt that sports and the Troy Strawberry Festival both represent his beloved city in the best possible light. In 2019, after nearly twenty-three years in the newspaper business, David left the *Troy Daily News* to become the director of communications for the Troy City Schools. I can truly call him a friend and supporter of the Troy community. He uses his journalistic talents to convey to the readers of this book the excitement of our Troy Strawberry Festival, its history and the many strawberry events that happen up to and during this first weekend in June.

I hope you enjoy reading *The Troy Strawberry Festival* and that this book will inspire you to visit the Troy Strawberry Festival in person. After you experience firsthand the sights, sounds, smells and, most importantly, the tastes of the Troy Strawberry Festival, you will understand author David Fong's passion for this annual event.

Happy reading!

—Michael L. Beamish
Mayor, City of Troy (2004–19)
Voice of the Troy High School Football Trojans

PREFACE

For decades, two things have marked the seasons in Troy, Ohio. In the quaint suburb tucked away nicely inside a bucolic landscape of corn and soybean fields, two passions have let its residents know when fall and summer started. Everyone knows it is not officially autumn until thousands of rabid high school football fans fill Troy Memorial Stadium to watch the Trojans play.

They also know the official kickoff to summer in Troy is not Memorial Day weekend but rather the very next week, the first weekend in June, when the smell of the Troy High School Music Boosters' strawberry donuts fill the air (with the donuts themselves filling the stomachs) and tens of thousands roam the downtown streets and levee along the Great Miami River as Troy rolls out the strawberry-red carpet for its annual Troy Strawberry Festival.

What began as a small festival in 1977 meant to bring the community together and raise money for community organizations and causes has grown into one of the largest not only in the state of Ohio but the entire Midwest. In 2018, *Ohio Magazine* readers voted it not only the state's "Best Food and Drink Festival" but also the state's "Best Summer Festival" in its annual readers' poll. That same year, the magazine named Troy one of the state's five "Best Hometowns."

And truthfully, the fact that despite its growth over the years—from around 10,000 in attendance that first year in 1977 to more than 150,000 in 2019—that "hometown" feel has remained a part of the festival's charm. While tens of thousands may descend upon Troy year after year that first full

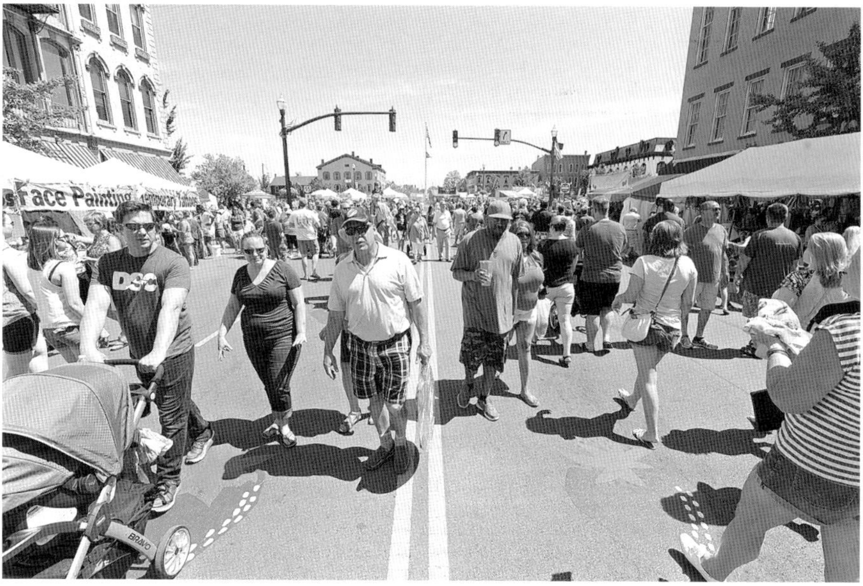

Thousands fill downtown Troy for the annual Troy Strawberry Festival. *Courtesy of the* Troy Daily News.

weekend in June, the Strawberry Festival has remained an event created and maintained by Trojans, for Trojans.

It is an event that allows local nonprofit organizations to find funding, some of which is enough to last the entire year. It's a place where Troy residents go to see and be seen. In some cases, people who may not have seen one another through an entire bone-chilling winter and soggy, windy spring are able to reunite under a gorgeous early summer sun while they munch on strawberry shortcake.

It's a place where your kids can compete in competitions, you can eat strawberry-flavored delights until your stomach aches and you can watch waves of people trek through your hometown.

As the world has swirled for more than four decades, the Troy Strawberry Festival has remained relatively constant. It's something people have come to count on every summer. It's like a friend waiting there to greet you one year since you last left it. It's a small-town piece of Americana that hasn't been overtaken by commercialism; it is still for the nonprofit organizations. It has continued to grow but still can be maintained and run by a large group of volunteers who share a vision and want to bring a gift to the people of Troy.

It's something Trojans never grow tired of, making their annual pilgrimage year after year.

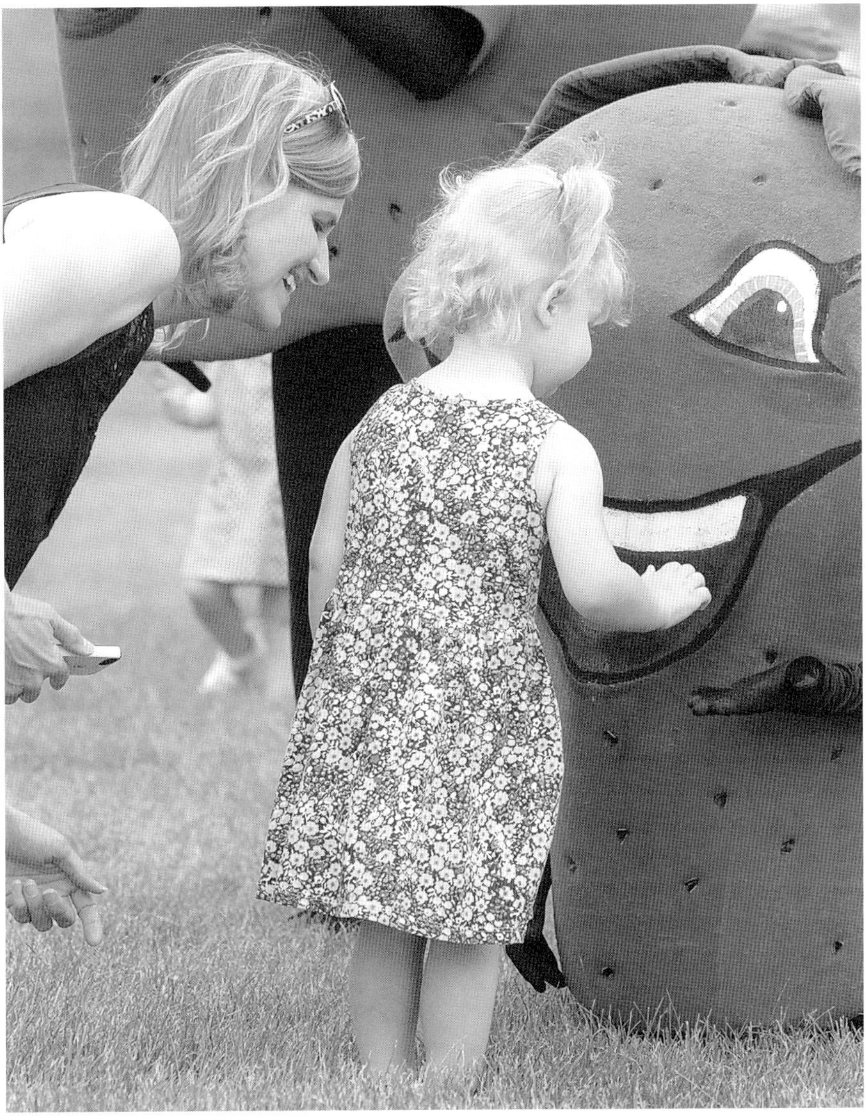

A young girl visits with the Troy Strawberry Festival mascot. *Courtesy of the* Troy Daily News.

The Troy Strawberry Festival also is something that has remained near and dear to my heart throughout the course of my life. I was born in 1973, the festival in 1977, so I suppose it is safe to say the festival and I have grown up, side-by-side, throughout the years.

At the first Strawberry Festival, employees from Friendly's Ice Cream concocted a one-hundred-foot-long strawberry shortcake for festivalgoers to enjoy. A few years later, Friendly's donated the ice cream and helped Troy High School's graduating seniors create a record-breaking ice cream sundae that would eventually make it into the pages of the *Guinness Book of World Records*.

Friendly's Ice Cream is actually what brought my family from Cincinnati to Troy when my father took a job in Troy's corporate offices in 1974. I still remember walking along the levee with my mom at the very first Strawberry Festival—my dad was tied up working in the Friendly's booth at the festival—in large part because I remember some sort of celebratory cannon fire. I was so startled by the noise that the cream soda I had been carrying ended up all over the front of my shirt.

All throughout my childhood, I remember my parents taking me, along with my five siblings—brothers Chris and Steve, sisters Julie and Jenny—to various festival events and competitions. One year, my brother Steven won the Strawberry Festival Super Kids competition, and we had to attend an awards ceremony later that night in the high school auditorium for him to receive his trophy.

At some point during the ceremony, inclement weather started rolling in and storms filled the sky (something that would be a common occurrence through the history of the festival, but we'll get to that). As we were preparing to leave, festival officials informed us a tornado had been spotted in the general area and we should remain inside the school until the danger had passed.

My mom took a quick inventory of her children, quickly realizing one had gone missing. My brother, clearly not one to take in the pageantry of the night, had left soon after he had received his trophy and was sitting in the family station wagon, waiting for the rest of us.

My mom sent my father down the hill to the car to get him and bring him back into the high school's sanctuary. According to a family legend that has since become apocryphal, they were halfway up the hill to the high school when my dad looked at my brother and said, "Where's your trophy?"

When my brother sheepishly informed my dad he had left it in the car, my father took one look at him and then—with a possible tornado bearing down on them—told him to go back to the car and get his trophy.

Never underestimate the power of Strawberry Festival baubles and trinkets.

We rarely missed the yearly parade through town, one of the events that has since gone by the wayside as Troy has continued to grow and evolve over the years. As a little kid, I was always thrilled that many of the organizations that marched through town passed out candy to the children along the parade route. As the parade wound down, my excitement reached a fever pitch as I saw two men dressed as clowns pushing a wheelbarrow and carrying shovels.

"Mom, look at that!" I exclaimed. "They have so much candy, they need a wheelbarrow and shovels to hand it out!"

"David," my mother said, trying to contain her laughter, "those are the guys who follow the horses in the parade and clean up their poop off the streets."

It was right around that time, at the tender age of about six, that I learned what the word *crestfallen* meant.

When I got to high school, I would spend the weekend hanging out at the festival with my two best friends, Eric Hughes and Randy Sentman. It gave us a nice break from our normal high school weekend routine, which largely consisted of unsuccessfully getting high school girls to talk to us.

In college, the Strawberry Festival was such a point of pride for me that I brought my college friends home from school that weekend to show off the town I loved so much.

After graduation, I started working at the *Troy Daily News*, where covering the festival in various forms became my job, although I always considered it a labor of love. It was at the *Troy Daily News* that one of my editors, David Kennard, asked me to join the company's bed-racing team.

For the next decade—perhaps spurred on by so many participation ribbons in Strawberry Festival Super Kids competitions—winning the Troy Strawberry Festival Bed Races became much more than a goal and something more akin to an obsession, not unlike Captain Ahab's lifelong hunt for the great white whale, Moby Dick.

With each passing year, I grew more desperate and my costumes for the event grew more outlandish, culminating with me getting a pink-and-green-dyed mohawk in 2010. Perhaps because I was more aerodynamic that year, perhaps because my fierce mohawk intimidated the other teams in the competition that year—or, more than likely, a lot of luck—I won the Troy Strawberry Festival bed races alongside my *Troy Daily News* teammates, Melanie "Twin" Yingst, Ron Osburn, Jim Davis and Anthony Weber. The very next year, we won it again, with my brother Steven filling in for an injured Ron Osburn.

There was no tornado, and my brother didn't leave his trophy in the car that year.

Now that I'm a little older, most of my Strawberry Festival priorities revolve around my children. Like so many others throughout the city I love, I am indoctrinating my children into the same tradition my parents introduced to me.

I want them to know this: Troy is the Strawberry Festival; the Strawberry Festival is Troy.

ACKNOWLEDGEMENTS

There are so many people I wish to thank for helping this book come to life. First, without my editor at Arcadia Publishing/The History Press, John Rodrigue, this obviously never would have happened. He helped me turn an idea about a local high school basketball team taking on LeBron James into a book about one of the largest festivals in the Midwest. Thank you and your publishing company for seeing the merit in this project.

Thank you to the Troy Chamber of Commerce and Troy Strawberry Festival committee members for putting on the best festival in the Midwest every year. Obviously with no festival, there is no book. I have loved the festival since I was a child, and that love has never once waned over the years. Thank you for the memories.

Troy Strawberry Festival manager Kathi Roetter gave me valuable insight into the inner workings of the festival. The Strawberry Festival is lucky to have someone with such passion leading the way every year.

The two men who were key to the birth of the Strawberry Festival were Steve Hamilton and Bill Fulton. Sadly, neither of them is with us any longer. I cannot possibly thank Kay Hamilton and Joyce Fulton enough for helping me understand their husbands' visions for the festival. They were both so kind and welcoming as they reflected on Steve and Bill.

I researched this book in the middle of a global pandemic, when most libraries were shut down. Thank you to local Troy librarians Rachelle Via and Patrick Kennedy for opening up your doors and letting me sneak in for a week to scour your files and your microfiche.

Acknowledgements

The remarkable photos in this book frequently tell a better story than I ever possibly could. Thank you to all those who donated, with a special thanks to the *Troy Daily News* (now *Miami Valley Today*) and *Dayton Daily News* for letting me use so many photos from your archives. The photos by Anthony Weber and Mike Ullery are stunning.

Spending twenty-two years working at the *Troy Daily News* helped me get a behind-the-scenes look at how the festival really works and how much work and preparation—most of which is done by volunteers—goes into creating a spectacle for more than 100,000 people. I was lucky to work with so many talented journalists over the years who continue to cover the festival to this day. Special thanks to Melody Vallieu and Josh Brown for helping me get access to your online archives.

I am no longer with the newspaper, having left in the summer of 2019 to become the Troy City Schools director of communications. Thank you to everyone in the Troy Board of Education offices for allowing me to pursue this side dream. And thank you to the many teachers who have over the years instilled in me a love of writing.

Whenever I needed to think through the next chapter in my book, I would go for a long walk to clear my head and think things through. Thank you to Scott Myers and the Miami County Parks District for providing the stunning backdrops against which I took these walks last summer and fall.

I spent most of my younger moments at the festival with my family members. I have many fond memories at the festival with Chris, Steven, Julie, Jenny and our adopted brother, Kevin Stewart.

My wonderful in-laws, David and Linda Olney, have delighted over the years in watching my children participate in various Troy Strawberry Festival events.

My parents took me to the festival every year. My father, Richard, passed away in 2015 and my mother, Jean, in 2019. I miss them every day and can't possibly thank them enough for all the support they gave me when they were still here.

Finally, and most importantly, I wouldn't be the writer or person I am without the love and support of my wife, Michelle, our daughter, Sophie, and our son, Max. They inspire me every day. Everything I do is for them. They can't possibly know how much they mean to me.

Chapter 1

THE BIRTH OF A FESTIVAL

It was a nut that ultimately caused a fruit to win out over a grain. And as a result, one of the most iconic traditions of a small town in southwest Ohio was born.

In 1976, Steve Hamilton was looking to start a festival in Troy, Ohio. After his parents had brought back a cherry and a brochure from a festival in Michigan, Hamilton, a member of the Troy Chamber of Commerce, was inspired to start a similar festival in his beloved hometown.

"Gee," Hamilton said in a 1982 interview with the *Troy Daily News*. "Troy ought to do something like this."

Hamilton then approached friend Bill Fulton, who—along with brother Tom—owned Fulton Farms in Troy, about the idea of holding a sweet corn festival the next fall. Fulton, who was a running enthusiast like Hamilton and had often run 10K races alongside his buddy, wanted to help but was unsure about the idea of a sweet corn festival—for one reason in particular.

Fulton, a graduate of The Ohio State University and a rabid Buckeye fan, was afraid a sweet corn festival held on a weekend in September might interfere with his ability to watch Ohio State play.

"He came home one evening and said that Steve wanted to have a sweet corn festival," said Joyce Fulton, Bill's widow. Bill Fulton passed away in 2016. "And I said, 'Really?' And he said, 'Well, that's what I thought. I told him he should do something in the spring. Everybody does things in the fall.' And Bill loved sports. He lived for football, basketball. His life started in September when the Buckeyes started playing football. I really believe he was worried about a festival getting in the way of him watching the Buckeyes play."

And that's how the Buckeyes—a football powerhouse named after a poisonous nut that falls from the buckeye tree—helped influence a Troy tradition that has been in place since 1977. What could have been the fall Troy Sweet Corn Festival became the Troy Strawberry Festival, to be held in early summer, when the strawberry crop is at its peak in Ohio.

Troy resident Carole Synan says she suggested the festival be named after strawberries, based on a strawberry festival she had visited in Humboldt, Tennessee, in the 1970s. After visiting that festival, she would suggest to Hamilton and the Troy Chamber of Commerce that the upcoming Troy festival be named after the red fruit.

"As a member of the Troy Jaycee Wives, I approached the group in November of 1976 about the idea for a strawberry festival in Troy," Synan said. "The ladies decided it was too big a project for the organization, so I took my idea to Lou Vlasho, who was the president of the Troy Chamber of Commerce at that time. He was very much interested in my proposal, and his interest helped make the idea become a reality. We obviously had the berries, and I also felt the festival had to include the well-attended arts and crafts show which had been in downtown Troy for a number of years.

"When the first planning meetings were held, the immediate interest from the nonprofit groups was very encouraging, and with support from the City of Troy, the festival planning moved forward at a fast pace. With Steve Hamilton taking on the responsibility as the first chairman, the first Troy Strawberry Festival came about within seven months of the first mention of it being a possibility. There is no doubt that his enthusiasm led to the success of the festival that first year and for many years that followed."

In the end, the decision to go with strawberries turned out to be the right one for a number of reasons. First and foremost, the Strawberry Festival had little to no competition from other festivals in early summer, while a fall festival would have put it around the same time as a number of other local and regional festivals.

Also, it certainly gave the local clubs and organizations selling food at the festival more options than corn likely would have. From common foods such as strawberry shortcake and chocolate-covered strawberries to more inventive fare such as strawberry cannoli and strawberry burritos, the little red fruit has proved a versatile ingredient. The Troy Music Boosters have sold, literally, millions of strawberry donuts throughout the history of the festival. It's hard to imagine the same thing happening with corn donuts.

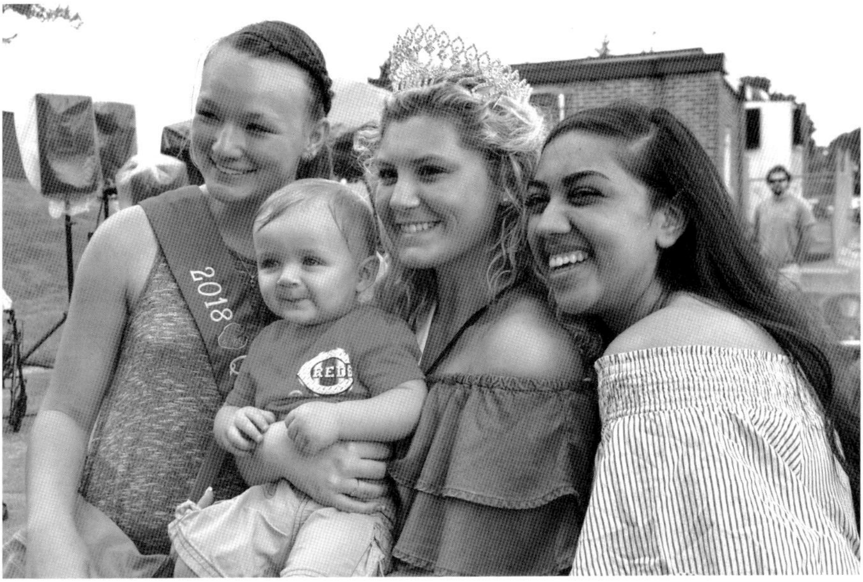

Troy Strawberry Festival Queen Brooke Klopfenstein (*center*) and members of her court pose with a baby. *Courtesy of the* Troy Daily News.

Finally, strawberries have turned out to be a bumper crop for Fulton Farms over the years. At the time the festival launched in 1977, the local farm was the largest producer of strawberries east of the Mississippi River.

"We had started out here with melons and sweet corn," Joyce Fulton said. "We didn't add the strawberries until probably around 1967 or so. It probably took around ten years or so for them to really take off. Bill was a dirt farmer. He had people from around the state who would come to him for advice and soil samples. He's in the [State of Ohio] Agricultural Hall of Fame. When the strawberries started to take hold out here, it was like the gold rush was on."

A bounty of fresh strawberries, coupled with a man with an abundance of vision and passion, led to the birth of the iconic festival. Once Hamilton had found his muse in the sweet fruit, he was off to the races.

"I had known Steve long enough and knew how committed he was to this town. He had a genuine love for this city, and he wanted to do something special for this city," said Kay Hamilton, Steve's widow. Steve Hamilton passed away from cancer in 2004 at the age of fifty-four. "He wanted to be able to do something that was going to put Troy on the map. Steve was always very energetic. He always represented Troy and was a very 'rah, rah, rah' Troy person."

"When Steve started this idea, I know he wanted to do something that would feature a local crop at Fulton's. So he contacted Bill, and they worked together. I believe corn was the first idea they came up with, but eventually they decided on strawberries. Looking back now, it's hard to imagine the Strawberry Festival being anything other than strawberries, but it was something that Steve and Bill really just worked out between the two of them, and I think everyone would agree it worked out for the best."

Once Hamilton had his idea fleshed out, his next step was getting the City of Troy on board. He met with city planner Steve Kalmar and city engineer Jim McGarry, who helped further put the plan into motion. The three agreed on one thing: they did not want to bring in a lot of outside companies and commercialize the event; rather, they wanted to keep it a mostly local festival that would benefit Troy and the surrounding area's nonprofit clubs and organizations.

"We did not want it to be a commercial thing," Steve Hamilton said in a 1982 interview with the *Troy Daily News*. "There would be no rides, for example, and it would help local clubs and organizations make money for their projects—so they wouldn't have to sell candy bars."

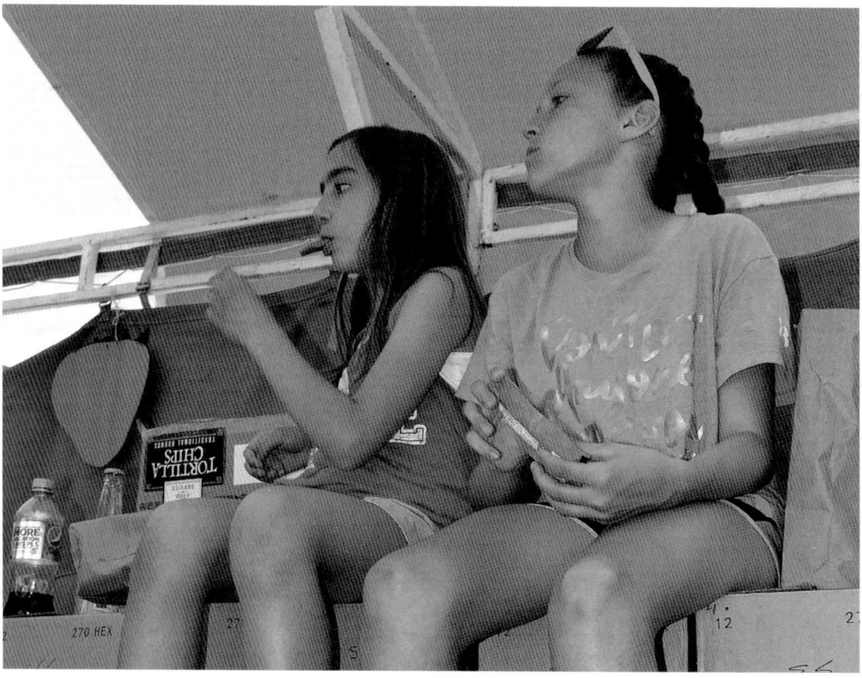

A pair of friends take in a show. *Courtesy of the* Troy Daily News.

Kay Hamilton, who would later work for the Troy Area Chamber of Commerce and was the festival's general manager for a number of years, said the concept of using the festival to give back to the community was very important to her husband.

"The clubs and organizations were definitely the backbone of the festival," she said. "They had to get behind it to make it happen. Steve wanted for the clubs and organizations to have a way to raise money. For some of them, it would become the only fundraiser they needed."

Initially, thought was given to holding the festival around the Miami County Courthouse or downtown Troy—an idea that would eventually be revisited in 2012 and become permanent in 2014—but ultimately it was decided to put the festival on the stretch of the Great Miami River levee between the Market Street and Adams Street Bridges.

Before this could happen, improvements had to be made to the levee, as the City of Troy put in electrical wiring, a paved ramp leading up the north side of the levee and a set of stairs on the south side of the levee. The improvements to the levee would continue with each passing year.

Kay Hamilton said the city's cooperation and involvement was crucial to the festival moving forward, not only during the early years but for every year moving forward.

"When he first brought the idea to the city, they absolutely embraced it," she said. "But that doesn't surprise me because of the type of person Steve was. He was very good about getting people to see his vision and getting them on board. That was so important, to get the support of the city, because of all the logistics involved in putting together a festival like the one Steve envisioned. We had to have the support of the city. Steve was such a positive person that when he went to the city officials, they were just infused by his enthusiasm."

It took Hamilton and a squadron of volunteers roughly nine months from the time they started planning in earnest to get the festival ready in time for its June launch.

Something else exciting was happening in the Hamilton household during that nine-month stretch, as well. "I was actually pregnant with Spencer right around that time," Kay said with a laugh. "He was born on May 30 [the first Strawberry Festival started on June 10], so I had to take him everywhere with me that first festival. Also at the time, my daughter Amy was going to Girl Scout camp, so I had to drive her out there, get back to the festival and watch Spencer, all at the same time. There wasn't a whole lot I could do, physically, because I just had Spencer, but I did what I could to help out. But at the time, it was definitely a very frenzied weekend, for a lot of reasons."

Even with all of the planning and preparation, Kay Hamilton said, no one was sure exactly what to expect from that first festival in 1977.

"We had been working on it so hard for so long that by the time it finally came time for the real thing, I didn't really know what to expect," Kay said. "We were shocked to see so many people and the way it came together. We were so lucky to have the volunteers we did who were willing to come together. A lot of that was Steve. He had a way of bringing people together. Troy is such a big family. Everything seemed to click, just like magic."

Including the weather. Over the years, the weather has played a crucial part in the degree of success of every Troy Strawberry Festival weekend, but it likely was more critical than ever that first year. Had it been washed out by rain that year, there's no telling if people would have bothered coming back the following year.

Fortunately, the festival had perfect weather both in 1977 and the second year, 1978. The festival did not see rain until the third year.

"We had perfect weather that weekend, which I think was very important. It was so important to get that festival started off the right way," Kay said. "If it had rained all weekend and everyone had stayed away or been slogging through the mud on the levee, it could have been a disaster. We had to give people a reason to want to come back the next year and then keep coming back every year after that."

Which, as it turns out, they did and they have. The festival has become a cornerstone of Troy culture, thanks in large part to two men who are no longer around to see what they helped create. Both of their widows, however, are proud to have their husbands associated with such a grand event.

"Bill was never one for the spotlight," Joyce Fulton said. "But it's nice to think we were there from the beginning and helped this become a regular thing for the city. We have been very blessed. We've had a blessed life."

Kay Hamilton said the festival has come to symbolize the love her late husband had for his hometown. "I think this is definitely a big part of his legacy, but he was also a businessman, he served on city council and he was a person who was always involved in his community," she said. "He was a guy who wanted to make his community a better place to live. That was just him. He was a man of vision. Steve was just such a likeable guy. He was so much fun and he was so smart, and he infused all of those things into the festival. He wanted to make sure everyone knew about his hometown and how much he loved his hometown."

Chapter 2

THE EARLY YEARS (1977–80)

1977

When the Troy Strawberry Festival made its debut on June 10, 1977, it did so to relatively little fanfare, even in the local newspaper.

The preview story in the *Troy Daily News* announcing the festival the day before it kicked off barely made the front page, as it was shoehorned into the lower right-hand corner, underneath a story about a grievance filed against the Miami County Jail's commissary.

"Honestly, nobody had any idea how big of a deal it would become," said lifelong Troy resident David Lindeman, who would spend more than two decades working for the *Troy Daily News*. "It just seemed like this idea some people had, and nobody knew if it would work or not. We didn't want to make too big of a deal out of it in the paper in case it wasn't around the next year. Those things happen sometimes. It got a little bigger the next year and a little bigger the year after that…and then over the years it grew into the huge deal that it is today."

One of the highlights of the first festival was the crowning of the festival queen the Friday night before the festival began. That honor went to Troy High School junior Patricia Ording, daughter of Mr. and Mrs. Alton Ording. Over the years, the festival would expand, and a number of "pre-festival" events would take place in the weeks before the actual festival in June. As such, the festival queen's pageant was eventually pushed back into the spring, giving future queens and their courts the opportunity to preside over the pre-festival activities.

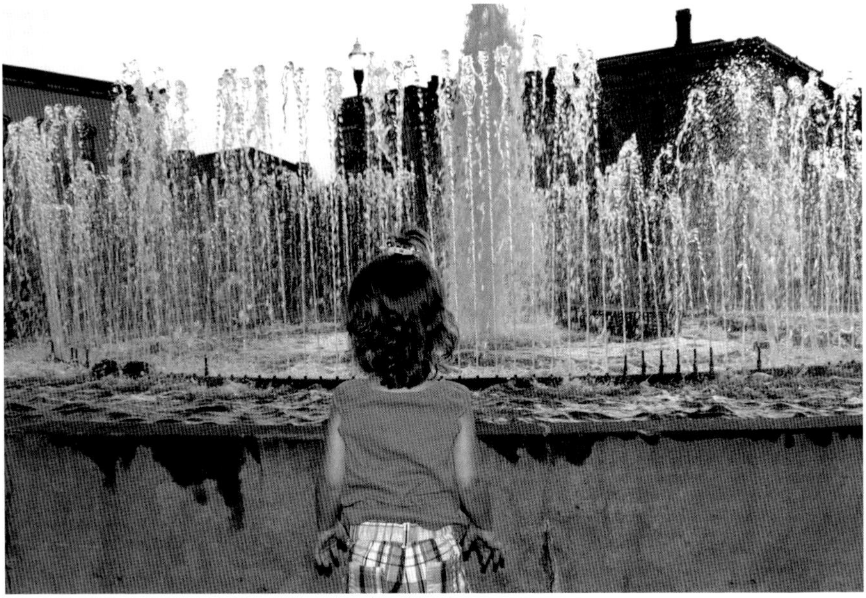

A young girl takes in the red dyed fountain in downtown Troy. *Courtesy of the Karnehm family.*

It would turn out to be a fairly low-key festival, especially when compared to what it would eventually grow into. One of the highlights of the first festival was supposed to be a Snoopy and the Red Baron hot air balloon launch, but a windy Saturday afternoon grounded that.

Other events that took place that weekend included a paper airplane contest, cloggers, aerobic dancers, a performance by the Piqua Water Ski Club and an appearance by several McDonaldland characters.

1978

The second annual Strawberry Festival built on the success of the first, featuring more food, more crafts, more performances, more booths and more competitions than its predecessor.

It also included additional electrical wiring on the levee and a set of steps to get from the river to the banks of the Great Miami River, both of which were maintained and improved upon in the years since, as those improvements become a year-round fixture.

"I think the improvements that were made really helped, particularly the electrical wiring on the levee and steps down to the riverbank," 1978 festival chairman Doug Trostle said in an interview with the *Troy Daily News*. "There was no problem getting around."

The 1978 festival also featured the debut of the Super Cities Competition, an event that would remain a fixture through much of the '80s before it eventually faded away with the passage of time, as many events have. In the Super Cities Competition, groups of residents from Troy and surrounding cities—Piqua, Tipp City, West Milton, Covington and Greenville joined in the first one—competed against one another in a series of obstacles and competitions.

"The city competition went really well," Trostle said in a *TDN* interview. "They really got into the spirit of the competition."

The competition got so heated that at one point a Troy councilman was eliminated from the competition with a dislocated knee.

1979

One of the biggest stories surrounding the 1979 Troy Strawberry Festival fell from the heavens above in the form of heavy rains throughout both days. That would become a recurring theme throughout the years, as inclement weather—everything from downpours to lightning strikes to tornado sightings—often played a large part in the festival's success. If you don't like the weather in Ohio, you can always wait a few minutes for it to change, the old saying goes.

While rain may have been coming down out of the sky, one thing that did not was the Greene County Parachute Sport Club, which was set to make an appearance at the festival but was unable to because of the weather.

The rain, however, did not keep more than forty-five thousand people from showing up that year.

"Everything went smoothly and it was really amazing—but we didn't have any problems," festival chairman Rick Jackson said. "Everyone cooperated with everyone."

One of the highlights from the festival was the introduction of the diaper derby, in which parents of young babies would try to coax their children to crawl twenty feet across a stage across a finish line. The diaper derby would become one of the festival's most-beloved events, one that has seemingly not seen its popularity wane over the years.

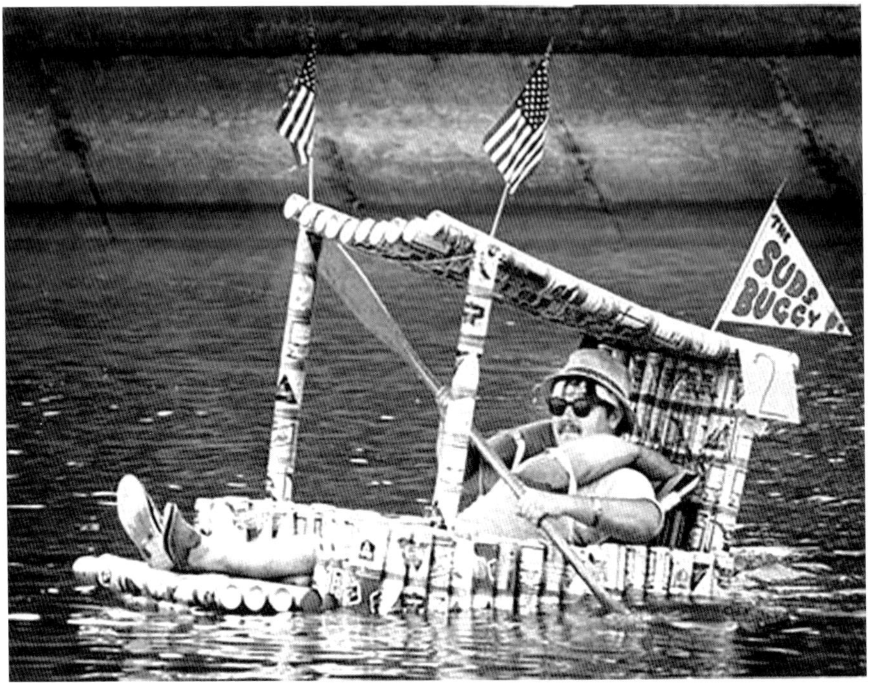

A man floats along during the Poor Man's Regatta during the early days of the Strawberry Festival. *Courtesy Mark Duncan/*Dayton Daily News.

1980

The 1980 Troy Strawberry Festival saw two major events happen—one that would change the course of the festival for decades to come and one that would put the festival in the *Guinness Book of World Records* for a period of time.

The first thing that happened under chairman Tom Thokey was the debut of a festival parade. This parade would remain a festival fixture until 2012, when it was put to a halt when the city completely replaced the Adams Street Bridge, meaning the city couldn't afford to close the streets used to host the parade due to safety concerns.

Also that year, the festival etched its name into the *Guinness Book of World Records* with the construction of, at the time, the world's largest ice cream sundae. On the field inside Troy Memorial Stadium, thirty Troy High School seniors, along with Friendly Ice Cream Corporation's donated ice cream, toppings and help from its employees, constructed a strawberry sundae that stood fifteen feet high and weighed in at 11,050

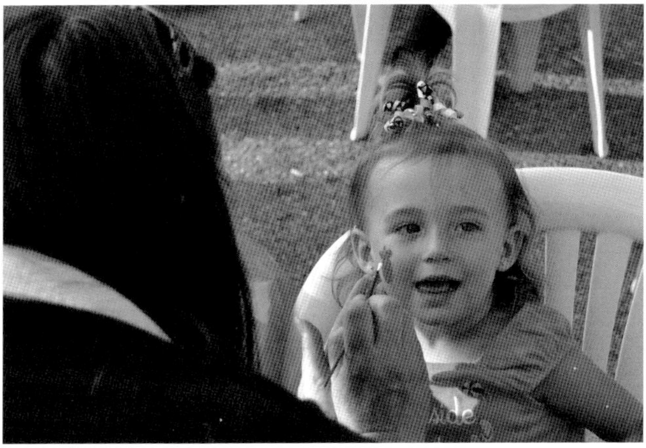

A young festival attendee gets a strawberry painted on her face. *Courtesy of the* Troy Daily News.

pounds, breaking the previous record by nearly 3,000 pounds. All told, the estimated calorie count on the sundae was 9,071,327.

Once the sundae had been completed, it was broken down and dished out to five thousand hungry onlookers.

Chapter 3

TROY LOVES A PARADE

So many events that would go on to become mainstays at the Troy Strawberry Festival sprang up from humble beginnings.

At 9:00 a.m. on Saturday, June 7, 1980, beginning at the town square in downtown Troy, the first-ever Troy Strawberry Festival Parade was born. The first festival featured twenty-one floats, four marching bands, five equestrian units, antique cars, firetrucks and horse-drawn wagons. The parade also featured twenty-two units from the Antioch Shrine in Dayton. The Shriners were the highlight of the parade that year, as they took twenty-two minutes to pass, with no units allowed in between them. The Shriners received twenty-nine requests to appear in parades that year, and the inaugural Troy Strawberry Festival Parade was one of the seven chosen.

High school marching bands from Troy, Newton, Bethel and Piqua appeared. Seventeen of the twenty-one floats—centered on the theme "A Family Affair"—were built by area civic clubs and organizations, while only four were professionally made.

Sure, it was a good start for a festival parade, but it was not nearly what it would eventually become, which was a two-hundred-unit parade that would become a featured broadcast on a regional television station in the Dayton area.

Some parade fans would show up before the son rose to stake out their favorite spots along the parade route. Others would show up the night before to place their lawn chairs—hoping they wouldn't be moved or tampered with overnight.

"I have been to every parade that ever happened," Stacy Westfall Hamilton said. "My mom took me to the first one. As I got older, we would walk uptown, and we always sat in the same spot, so we would be uptown by 5:30 a.m. We would get donuts at the bakery downtown. When they closed, we then had to go down to Tim Hortons. One year I sat in a different location, and as the parade was ending, the police and EMS showed up at the house I was sitting in front of that morning. Later I found out it was an awful scene of a murder-suicide. I then went back to my normal parade location and sat there every year until they killed the parade. We would also record the parade at home and then see if we made it on TV."

In fact, it was television that helped the parade grow exponentially. Soon after WHIO Channel 7 began broadcasting the parade every year, more and more groups wanted to be a part of the show, many with hopes of ending up on television.

"With Channel 7 broadcasting the parade, it attracted quality parade units from all over and spectators along the parade route," said retired Channel 7 Northern Bureau chief Steve Baker. "Jim Baldrige, Cheryl McHenry, Bruce Asbury were the WHIO talent in the early years, and the Troy Strawberry Festival Committee provided an on-air person. A lot of times it was Joe Mahan. Charlene Swob also did it. I worked 'on the street' doing on-air interviews with the various parade units. A few times I helped judge floats prior to the parade."

Baker said sometimes other festivals in the area would use the broadcast to draw attention to their own festivals. "The following weekend [after the Troy Strawberry Festival] was Versailles Poultry Days," Baker said. "They always had the big plastic blown-up chicken, with the Poultry Days Queen and Little Miss Poultry Days, in the Troy Strawberry Festival Parade. One year, they brought us barbecue chicken dinners and gave them to us to use live on TV—a great gimmick on their part—but they still won't give me the recipe for the barbecue chicken! To this day they still won't tell me.

"I would do a story the following weekend for Poultry Days. My favorite line in my story would be, 'Last weekend the strawberry was king in Troy, this weekend the chicken is the king in Versailles, which was once the poultry capital of the world.'"

Baker said that while the coverage was always well received, there was a lot of work behind the scenes that went into bringing the story to the masses over the airwaves every year. He said his wife, Marty—a longtime Troy City Council member and former prudent of council—would make sure there were fresh strawberries, strawberry donuts and other strawberry treats for the Dayton crew on the reviewing stand where the talent sat during the parade.

"It took a behind-the-camera crew of about five people, plus a large live truck used to control the parade coverage, switching cameras and calling the shots," Baker said. "I watched the parade one year from a hospital bed at Upper Valley Medical Center. I had been hospitalized the night before. Hospital staff would stop into my room to get a glimpse of the parade on TV."

Sometimes, the talent from the Channel 7 news team would get a "lift" covering the parade. "My dad used to bring his bucket truck and put it on the square and let Channel 7 get up in the truck and film the parade," Jody Liddy said. "I remember a very young Jim Baldridge and very young Cheryl McHenry. My dad was Jim Montgomery and owned Montgomery Tree Service. He did that every year for a while. The parades were fabulous. I really miss them."

For some, the memories of the Troy Strawberry Festival Parade are forever tied to their childhood of friends, family and pets.

"It was 1985. I was living on Ross Street over by Ording's [restaurant]," Tommy Dotson said. "I was twelve years old at the time. After we had subs and wedges, I got dressed and got my dog Charlie in the backyard. We walked up the hill as a shortcut. We walked down the unused railroad tracks up to the bridge that used to be by Ording's with an underpass. We walked down the hill, and Charlie and I sat down in the street and the four-way intersection by the old Troy Lumber Company Building.

"With a bottle of Pepsi and Charlie by my side, we sat there and watched the Strawberry Festival Parade. My pal Charlie and I had a great time. That day is still dear to my heart. Charlie lived until 2003. Charlie was old and sick at the end, but I sat with him on his last day, just as I did that warm summer day watching the parade. That's my Strawberry Festival memory that I'll always treasure."

One of the highlights of the parade was always the selection of the parade grand marshal, typically a Troy dignitary, celebrity or someone who had contributed to the community over the years. Former festival chairwoman Roberta Jacobs fondly remembers the year she ran the festival and popular Troy mayor Pete Jenkins was the grand marshal.

"One of my highlights of TSF was 2003, when I was chairperson and Pete Jenkins was grand marshal," she said. "He embraced the role with enthusiasm and positivity in 'Pete' fashion."

Some families would participate in the parade in different units over the years.

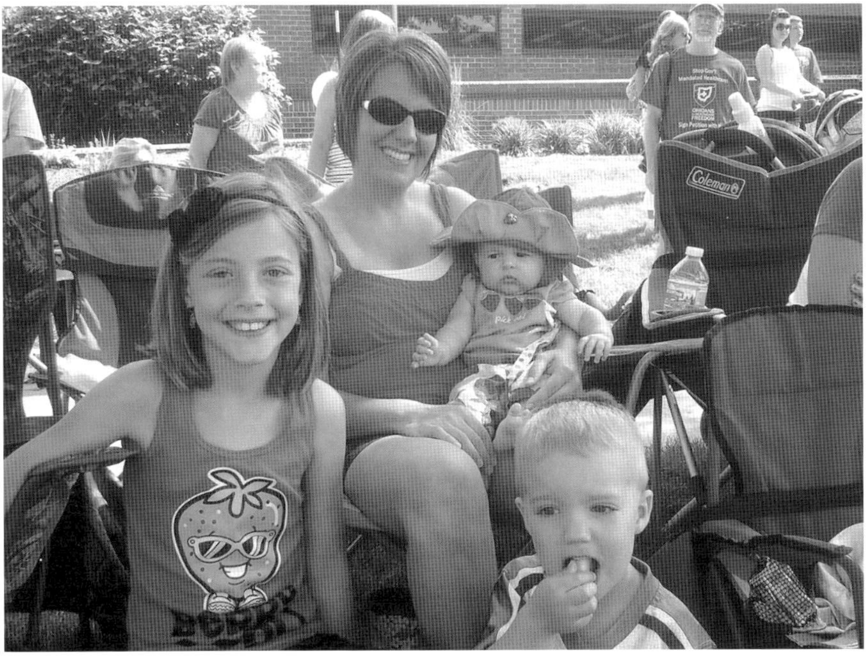

The Brogan family watches the Troy Strawberry Festival Parade. *Courtesy of Erica Brogan.*

"My dad was part of Corvette Troy and was in the parade yearly; he also entered the annual car show," Darla Renee Goodin said. "I've been in the parade as well with the Miami East Marching Band, twice playing my clarinet and twice as drum major."

The parade was not without its glitches, of course. As is the case with so many other events during the Strawberry Festival the first week of June, weather could play a big part in the success or failure of the parade. Sometimes, it rained on their parade.

"In 1990, I was a banner holder in the parade," Michelle Moore said. "It downpoured, and I was with the other girl on the very last banner. My parents were watching the parade from home, and apparently, the TV crew caught my sour face, which was a result of being soaked to the bone, broadcasting it for everyone to see."

At some point during the parade's long history, its path became lined with strawberries. A few nights before the parade, the streets along the route would be closed down, allowing "berry fairies"—groups of festival volunteers, usually including that year's Strawberry Festival queen and her court—to paint giant strawberries on the roadways.

"I remember the Wednesday before the Strawberry Festival, the police would mark off Market and Main Streets where the parade route was, and we would start about 9:00 p.m. and there we were, crawling down Market and Main Streets painting strawberries on the street and in front of businesses," Brian Wilgus said. "We would finish like midnight or a little after. Then a bunch of us would go to the old Steak N Shake here in Troy to eat. It was so much fun."

Another parade favorite were the Strawberry Festival mascots that walked along the parade route and could be spotted roaming the festival grounds throughout the weekend.

"When the festival started the fair berries, I was the first to wear the berry that year," Sandy Jean Smith Hall said. "I went to most of the events and had my photo taken with McGruff the Crime Dog. They had not put the protection on the costume, so every time it looked like rain, I got put in a tent. My husband and children made sure I got to the places I needed to be. We had such a great time."

While the parade consisted mostly of local and regional units, one year a nationally recognized unit joined in the parade. In 2005, the world-famous Anheuser-Busch Clydesdales were the featured unit in the Troy Strawberry Festival Parade. On April 22 of that year, one eight-horse hitch left New York City and another hitch left San Francisco as part of a twenty-one-city nationwide "Here's to the Heroes Tour 2005." Troy was the only Ohio city

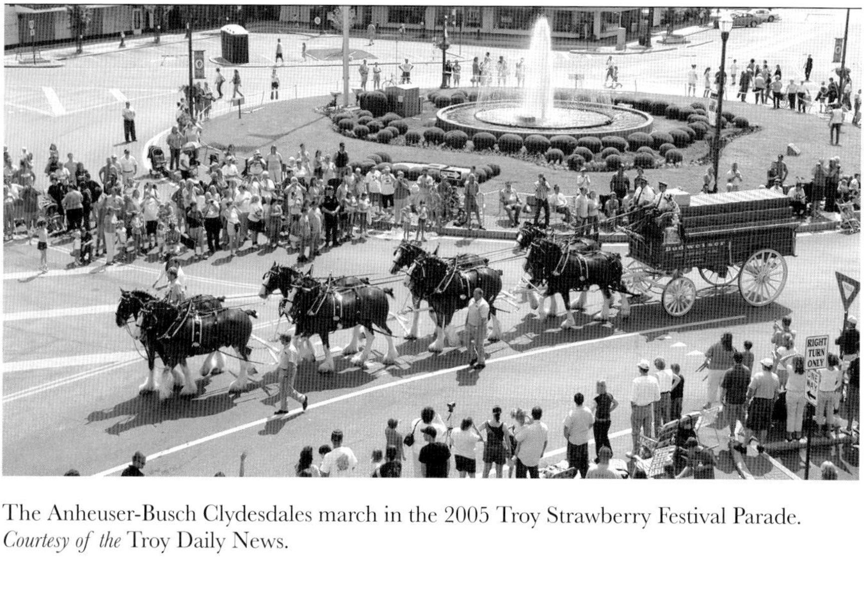

The Anheuser-Busch Clydesdales march in the 2005 Troy Strawberry Festival Parade. *Courtesy of the* Troy Daily News.

selected to be a part of that tour. Bringing the famed Clydesdales to Troy was no easy task, as it took years of putting in requests and planning.

"As parade chairman, you always try to bring something big to the event," 2005 parade chairman Jody Davis said in an interview with the *Troy Daily News*. "It took us about 10 years to pull this off, but we finally got the Clydesdales to Troy. And being a part of the 'Here's to the Heroes' tour is quite an honor that Anheuser-Busch has bestowed upon us."

The Clydesdales were housed at the Miami County Fairgrounds in the days leading up to the parade. Also at the fairgrounds was a fifty-three-foot-long red-and-gold tractor-trailer that opened up into an interactive experience, giving community members the opportunity to learn about Anheuser-Busch's 150-year legacy of support for the military. Thousands showed up at the fairgrounds, not only to see the famed horses, but also to send messages of support to the troops.

"This is wonderful for us," Diana Thomson, executive director of the Miami County Visitors and Convention Bureau, said. "We're thrilled that Anheuser-Busch has placed this prestigious exhibit in our community. It's great exposure for us and it just adds to the excitement of the festival."

It turned out the Clydesdales would be a massive boon to the parade and the festival itself.

"They brag they bring an extra 25,000 people wherever they go," Davis said. "I think it is a pretty big deal. How many times do you get the famous Clydesdales to come to Troy?"

At the time, no one could have possibly known it, but that would be one of the final highlights of the Troy Strawberry Festival Parade.

In 2012, the Adams Street Bridge—which, along with the Market Street Bridge, bracketed the section of the Great Miami River levee that had hosted the festival since its inception in 1977—was closed for repairs. As a result, that year the festival was taken off the levee and moved to downtown Troy, right in the middle of the parade route. That year, there was no Troy Strawberry Festival Parade.

"Obviously, we were genuinely sad about that," said former festival general manager Heather Dorsten in an interview with the *Troy Daily News*. "But we promise the festival will be back next year."

The festival would return to the levee in 2013, reviving the parade.

"We are so happy to have the parade back again," Dorsten said in a *Troy Daily News* interview that year. "People were very disappointed we didn't have a parade last year. There were some people who actually came out Saturday morning because they didn't realize or hadn't heard we

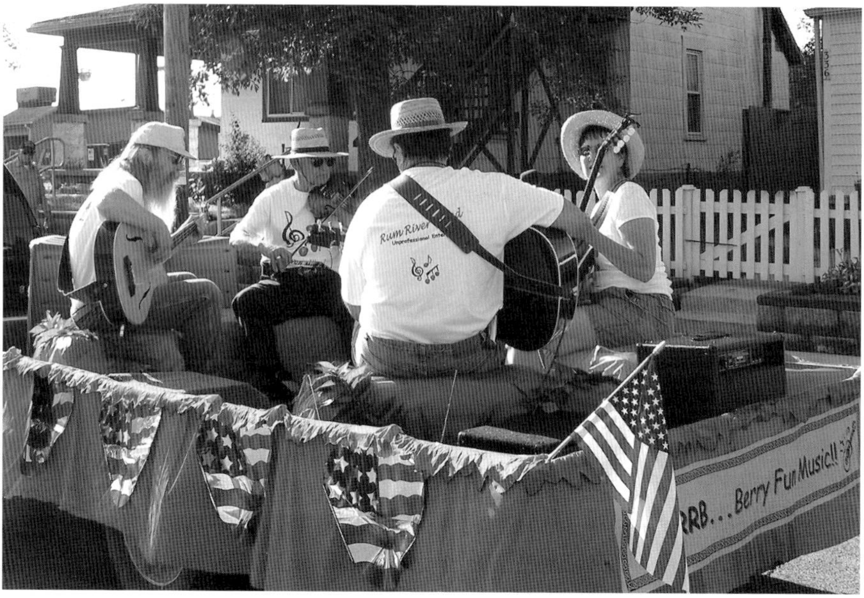

Rum River Blend rides along in the Troy Strawberry Festival Parade. *Courtesy of Linda Tartarian.*

weren't having a parade last year. I was helping set something up Saturday morning, and when I went around the corner, I saw people setting up chairs for the parade.

"People are very excited the parade is coming back this year. We've had a lot of people calling and asking if they could turn in their application late, because they didn't realize the parade would be coming back this year."

As things would turn out, however, the parade would return for just one year before it was gone again. In 2014, the Troy Strawberry Festival—which realized some of the merits in holding the festival downtown in 2012—would split the festival between two locations, hosting some booths and events on the levee and some in downtown Troy. With the festival again in downtown Troy, there was no parade route.

Current festival manager Kathi Roetter said that in the latter years before it was eliminated, the parade had started to lease steam anyway. Shutting it down when the festival moved to downtown may have happened on its own eventually.

"I think that if you grew up here, there were years that the parade was top-notch. And then, there were some years towards its end that it really was just concrete trucks," Roetter said. "All the things we had in the 1980s and

1990s, all of the floats and those sorts of things, they were gone. People just weren't as interested as they had been.

"And then Channel 7 wasn't interested in broadcasting it anymore. They actually had pulled out. The volunteers at the time had looked for other options, and it just didn't work out. So without that, then you have to start looking at the expenses of a parade. And there are expenses that people are not aware of. So it just didn't make sense. I will say that every time a vision committee meets or there is any kind of strategic planning, it's always discussed. I mean, it's always front and center. 'What can we do differently to have a smaller parade?' So if there's going to be an event that comes back, that would probably be the one."

There has not been another Troy Strawberry Festival Parade.

While the parade appears to be gone forever or at least the foreseeable future, the memories remain for many. "I loved marching in the parade," said former Troy High School marching band field commander Sarah Burk, a 1992 Troy High School graduate. "I have a lot of fond memories of the festival and the parade, especially seeing my friends there along the parade route."

Chapter 4

THE FESTIVAL GROWS, EXPANDS (1981–86)

1981

The story of the 1981 festival was the weather.

Somewhere between 80,000 and 100,000 people were forced home early the Saturday afternoon of the festival when heavy storms rolled into the area. Things would calm down later in the evening, only to have things pick up again that night. Three separate tornadoes were spotted in the area over the course of the night, although none came close enough to Troy to do any damage to the festival.

"Luckily, the weather improved and the crowds came back Sunday," festival chairwoman Charlene Walther said in an interview with the *Troy Daily News*. "By noon, the levee was packed shoulder-to-shoulder."

Perhaps fittingly, that year the Miami County Amateur Radio Club won the award for Best Event, for its constant monitoring of the weather conditions Saturday and Sunday.

"Without them, we could have had a real tragedy Saturday," Walter said. "You can't overestimate their contribution."

1982

One year after heavy storms and tornado sightings forced a shortened Strawberry Festival, it rebounded in a big way with perfect weather and record-setting crowds as an estimated 160,000 people flooded into Troy.

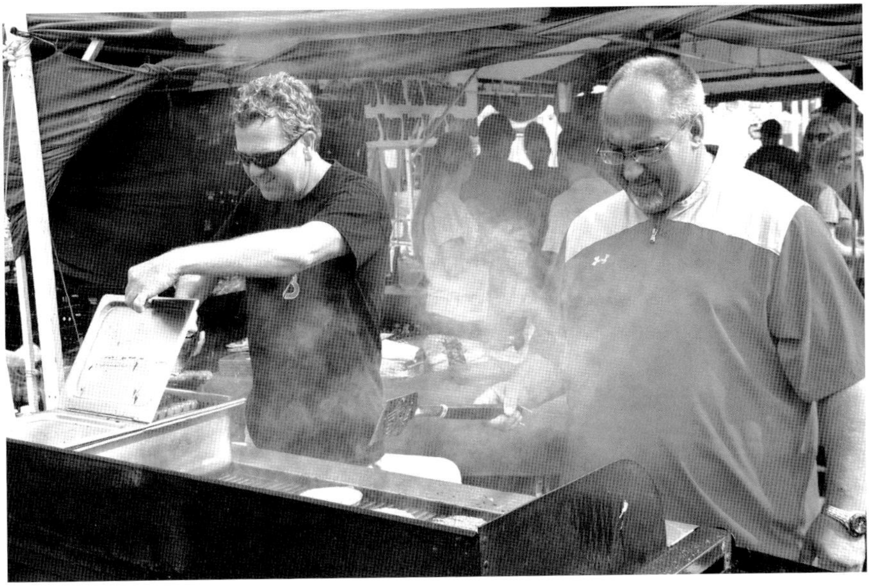

Working the grill at the Troy Strawberry Festival. *Courtesy of the* Troy Daily News.

"Everything went very well," festival publicity chairwoman Charlene Walther said. "Strawberry Shortcake was a delight for the children. There were lots of good comments about the parade, especially the Tipp City Jaycees lawnmower drill team. We had 824 entries in the Strawberry Classic, 200 more than last year, and booths were selling out of food by mid-afternoon Sunday."

Another highlight of the weekend was the crowning of Spencer Hamilton, son of acknowledged Troy Strawberry Festival founder Steve Hamilton, as Little Mister Strawberry.

1983

The Strawberry Festival featured a new exhibit this year with the Manufacturers' Expo at Hobart Arena, located just to the north, a parking lot away from the festival's traditional home on the levee. Roughly two thousand visitors per hour walked through the arena and were able to see the exhibitions set up by Edison State Community College and the chambers of commerce from Troy, Piqua, Tipp City, West Milton and Covington.

Once again, the festival had good weather as organizers began looking at ways for the festival to grow in the coming years.

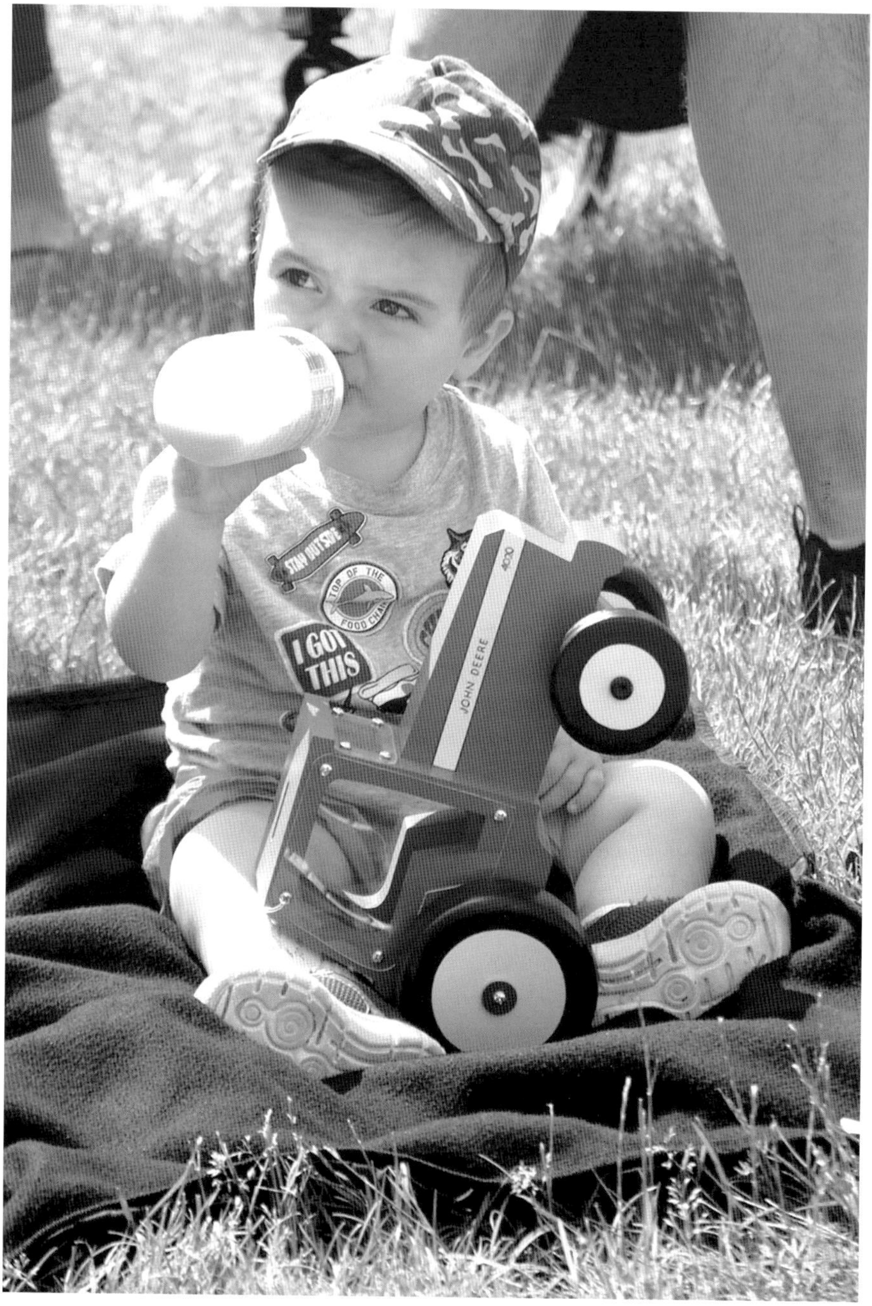

A young festivalgoer takes a drink while relaxing. *Courtesy of the* Troy Daily News.

"There are so many avenues and ways we can grow," festival chairman Malvern Timm said in an interview with the *Troy Daily News*. "But we have to be careful so it does not get out of hand. We have a tremendous facility, but it is too small in some respects."

1984

Late in the summer of 1984, the United States hosted the Summer Olympics in Los Angeles. Earlier in the summer, Troy was feeling the Olympic spirit with its "Go for the Berries" theme.

Much like the Americans did in an Olympics that was heavily boycotted by Communist nations, the Troy Strawberry Festival set records that year in terms of attendance, despite temperatures in the nineties throughout the weekend.

"It's just fantastic," chairman Earl Burley said in an interview with the *Troy Daily News*. "We feel we probably broke the record for attendance about 2:30 [Sunday afternoon]. An estimate is hard to make, but we've exceeded any previous record."

As a result of the large crowds, many food booths had to shut down before the festival reached its conclusion Sunday evening because they had sold out of their wares.

1985

One thing that has been a constant through the history of the Troy Strawberry Festival, from its early days right through the present, is innovation. Every general chairperson attempts to put his or her own spin on things. Some events or activities are one-and-done. Some have become staples and it's hard to imagine the festival without them. Some will go away and come back years later.

In 1985, the festival debuted a pair of new events. One was Troyathlon, a swimming, biking and running event. The other was the first-ever concert in Troy Memorial Stadium during the festival, which featured country/rock group McGuffey Lane. An estimated 4,500 fans showed up for the concert.

"I haven't heard anything in the way of complaints this year that I'd even care to remark on," festival chairman Steve Kalmar said. "It is almost unnerving to see it so smooth."

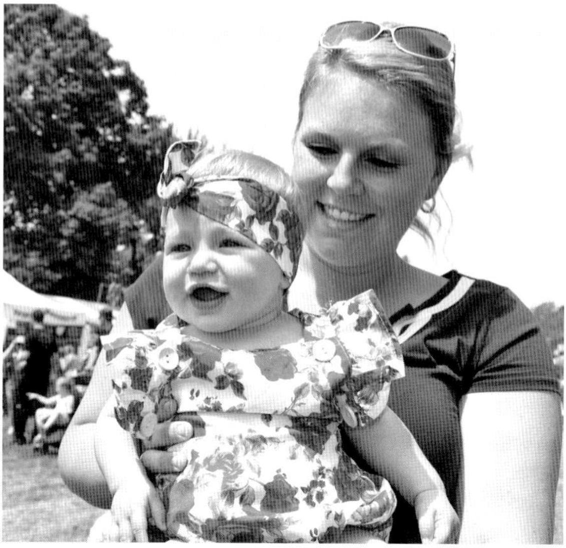

A family enjoys the Strawberry Festival. *Courtesy of the* Troy Daily News.

1986

The festival nobody was certain would make it much past its first year celebrated in 1986 with the tenth annual Troy Strawberry Festival.

Heavy rains were scheduled to dampen the weekend's proceedings, but aside from a heavy shower that shut things down for about an hour on Saturday, the festival was well attended as it turned ten.

"Every event in the festival came off as planned," festival chairman Tim Lanahan said in an interview with the *Troy Daily News*. "All the advance planning and organization paid dividends. I've heard nothing but very positive comments. I traveled to many of the booths, and the concession people all said they have done very well this year."

Chapter 5

FRIDAY NIGHT FUN

By 1986, less than a decade after its inception, the Troy Strawberry Festival was practically bursting at the seams, yearning to break free from its Saturday–Sunday constraints. That year, the festival grew by one day, as a Friday Night Kickoff event was added to the annual lineup.

"I think it happened for a lot of reasons," said former Troy Strawberry Festival manager Kay Hamilton. "Probably the biggest reason it happened was for the downtown businesses. For so many years, they had watched people go to the festival on the levee, but how many people were coming across the river to shop downtown? I thought having a Friday Night Kickoff event was an excellent idea."

Not only did adding Friday night to the proceedings help out the downtown Troy businesses, but it also helped build excitement for the upcoming festival the next two days, current Troy Strawberry Festival manager Kathi Roetter said.

"It was really important," Roetter said of the Friday Night Kickoff event. "That was a celebration, the hometown celebration, as we like to call it. It kind of felt like the countdown on New Year's Eve. There was just a buzz to it. You could feel it downtown. Also, we have so many people who are working at the nonprofits all weekend, that Friday night gave them the opportunity to come downtown, enjoy and celebrate our community and the festival itself. "Also, for the smaller nonprofits that weren't able to man a booth all weekend, they could come and fundraise, selling hot dogs, slices of pizza, whatever it may be."

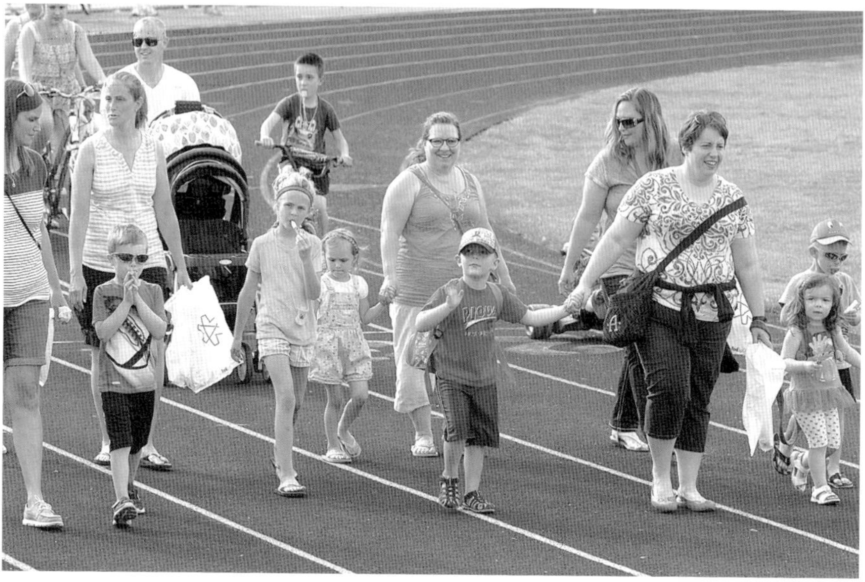

Children walk around the track inside Troy Memorial Stadium during the Friday night children's parade. *Courtesy of the* Troy Daily News.

There were several events that became synonymous with the Friday Night Kickoff: dyeing the water in the downtown fountain red, the bed races, the kids big wheel races and the car show and cruise-in.

In particular, the bed races seemed to capture the imagination of Troy residents. In the event, one driver would sit on a bed equipped with wheels, while four teammates pushed it down Market Street and halfway around the downtown fountain. Once they were halfway around, the driver would hop off the bed and the team would have to engage in some sort of wacky stunt—many of which involved them getting wet or messy—and then the driver would hop back on the bed and the teams would sprint toward the finish line.

Most of the teams were made up of participants from different businesses around town and competed in the open (co-ed) division, male division or female division. Literally thousands would line the streets and sideways in downtown Troy to watch the event.

"The bed races were a huge deal," Roetter said. "People absolutely loved them. It really helped build the excitement for the festival. It was just a festive atmosphere downtown. Toward the end, however, we started getting less and less teams because a lot of the companies that had once supported the event didn't want their employees participating anymore. It got so competitive and people were getting hurt—never anything serious—competing in the bed races. People were missing work because of bed race injuries."

When the festival moved all of its events downtown in 2012 as a result of the Adams Street Bridge closing, the bed races were moved to the Hobart Arena parking lot, but attendance was sparse. When the festival moved downtown permanently in 2014, both the bed races and car show and cruise-in were eliminated altogether.

"We found in 2012 that the bed races just weren't the same," Roetter said. "There wasn't the same atmosphere. It wasn't the same watching people race around a parking lot as it had been watching them race around the square. People didn't come out to watch it."

Roetter said she still gets asked about both the bed races and car show and cruise-in, along with the Saturday morning parade. "The three things I get asked about the most are, without a doubt, the bed races, the parade and cruise-in," she said. "Those are the top three, and it's not even close. Unfortunately, the bed races and parade probably aren't coming back, for a variety of reasons, at least for the foreseeable future. We are looking at a way to bring back the car show and cruise-in in some capacity. We don't know what that will look like just yet, but it is definitely something we'd like to do."

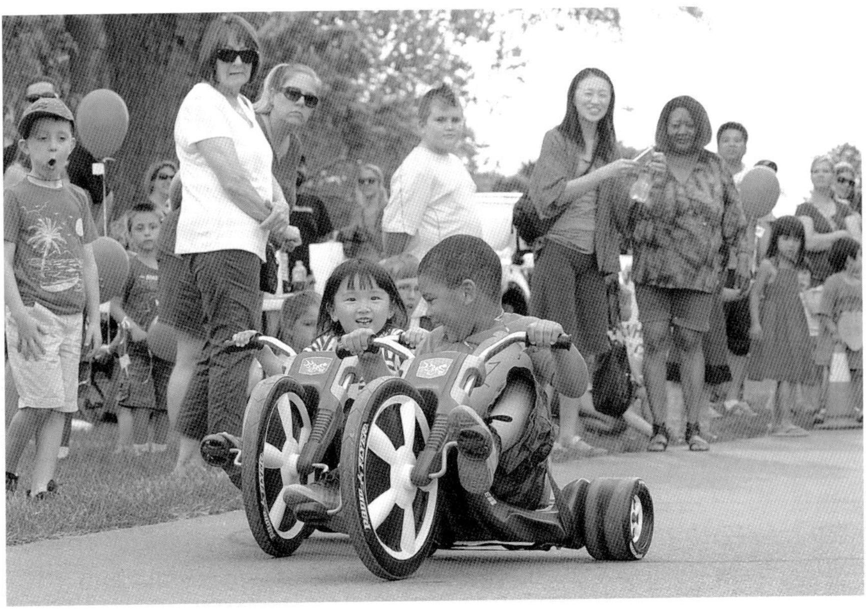

A crowd watches the big wheel races. *Courtesy of the* Troy Daily News.

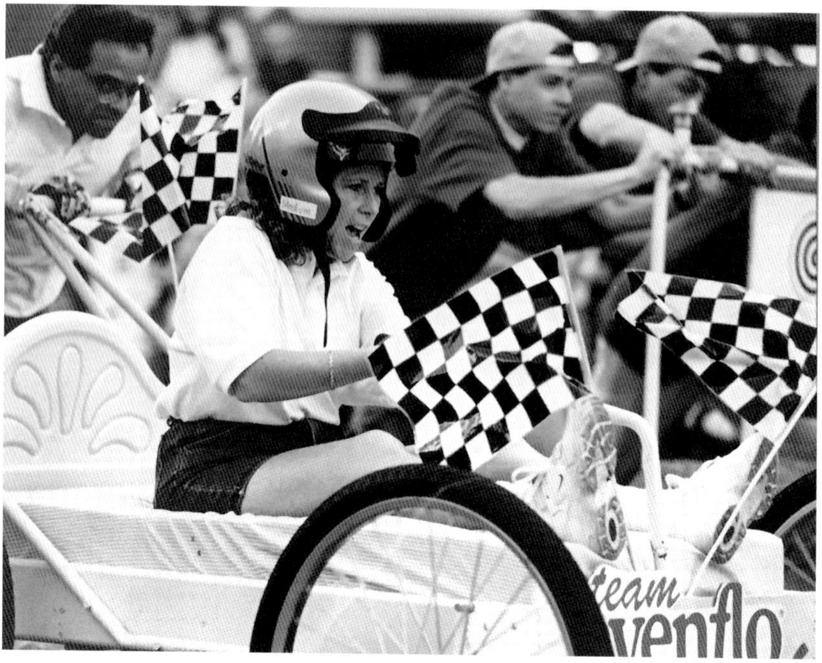

The Evenflo team competes in the bed races. *Courtesy of Martha Herrick Bravo.*

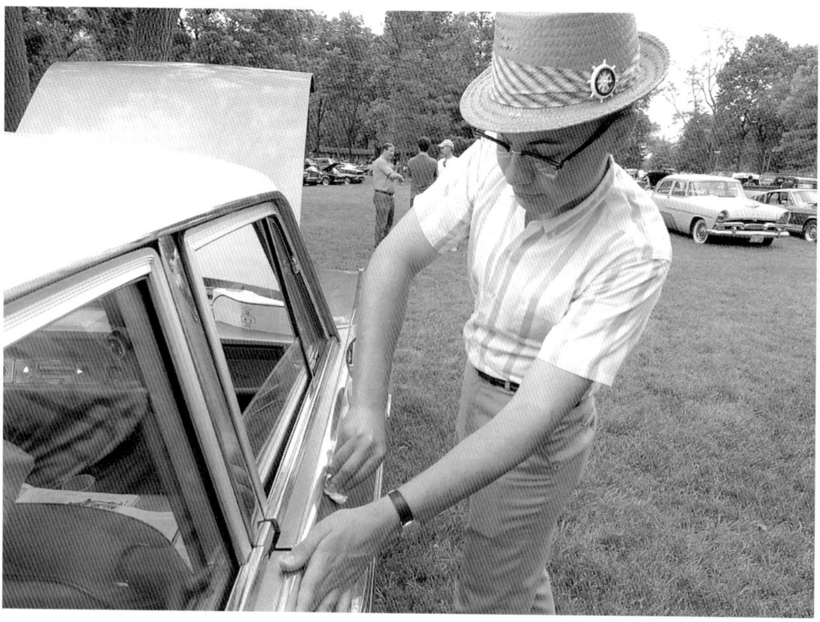

A car show participant gets his vehicle ready. *Courtesy of the* Troy Daily News.

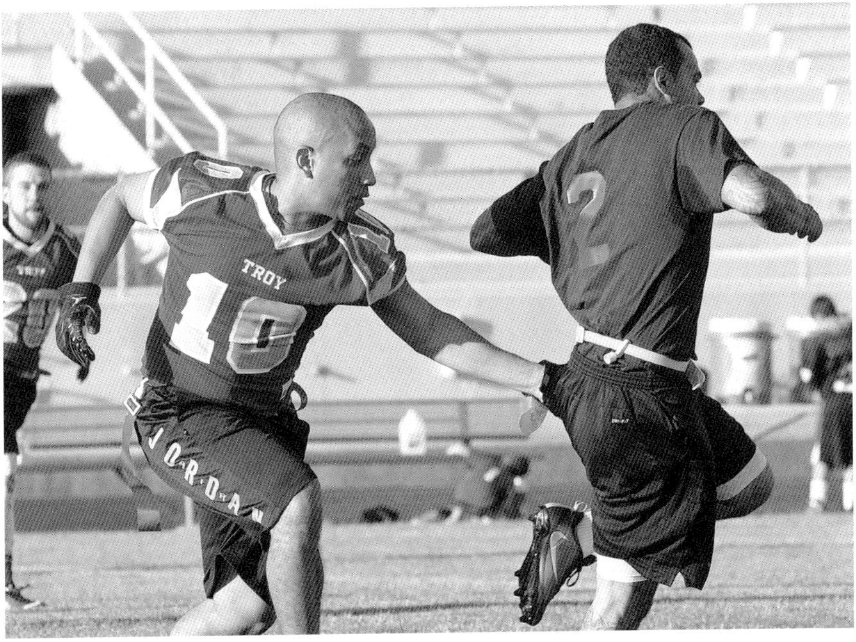

Dymond McDonald (*left*) grabs the flag of a Piqua player during the annual Troy-Piqua Alumni Flag Football Game. *Courtesy of the* Troy Daily News.

While the bed races and car show may be gone, the Friday night events continue. The festival committee has tried to add different events to entertain the crowd, which still shows up on the eve of the festival. In addition to events downtown, there are also events at the amphitheater at Treasure Island in Troy. There are more entertainers than in years past, and the Troy-Piqua Alumni Flag Football Game now takes place at Troy Memorial Stadium on the Friday night before the festival.

"Since we had to take away some things, we've definitely tried to add some things," Roetter said. "We want it to still be something that gets people in this community excited for the festival."

As things would turn out, holding a Friday Night Kickoff in downtown Troy served as a dress rehearsal of sorts for when the festival moved downtown for one year in 2012 and then permanently in 2014. In the end, Roetter said, it proved to be a tremendous benefit for all of downtown Troy.

"We had heard that people had no clue," Roetter said. "So, we are dyeing that fountain red and the visitors that come had no clue. They were not driving downtown because they favored taking the shuttle. They were coming to Staunton or to Adams and then just going in the venue. So, people

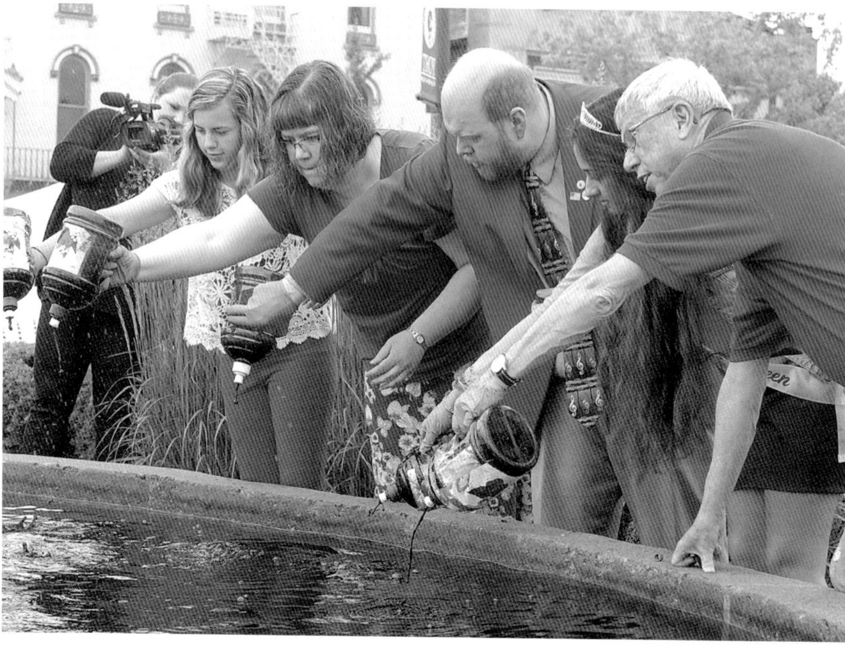

Festival officials pour dye into the fountain as part of the Friday Night Kickoff activities. *Courtesy of the* Troy Daily News.

weren't coming downtown. So not only were they not seeing our gorgeous red fountain that weekend, they also were not seeing our downtown and not having the opportunity to, hopefully, see some shops and restaurants that they weren't going back to. So that was the other thing. How can we—since the chamber manages the Strawberry Festival—how can we make this work for business but also still keep the nonprofits front and center? And we think we've found a way to do that. It's been great for downtown Troy and it's been great for the festival. It's not just a Friday night thing anymore. It's the entire festival."

Chapter 6

CLOSING OUT THE 1980s (1987–89)

1987

Hot air balloons filled the skies above the Strawberry Festival to open the event in 1987.

The festival also continued to make use of Hobart Arena, as it introduced a Saturday night Christian rock concert and, capitalizing on one of the hot trends at the time, a Trivial Pursuit competition, which was won by a team of Troy educators: Rick Thorpe, Billy Joe Emerick, Neil Chapman and Dennis Dyke.

At the annual Diaper Derby, Troy sports fans got a sign of things to come many years later from Levi Fox. Seventeen years later, Fox would show his speed on a different track, winning an Ohio High School Athletic Association Division I state championship in the 3,200-meter run.

"It was an excellent festival," chairperson Jan Manning said in an interview with the *Troy Daily News*. "Our slack times were not slack this year. It was one of the biggest crowds we ever had."

1988

Before he ran a city, Mike Beamish ran the Strawberry Festival.

In 1988, Beamish, who would go on to serve more terms as mayor of Troy than anyone else ever elected to that position, served as chairman of the festival. Under his guidance, the festival was a rousing success.

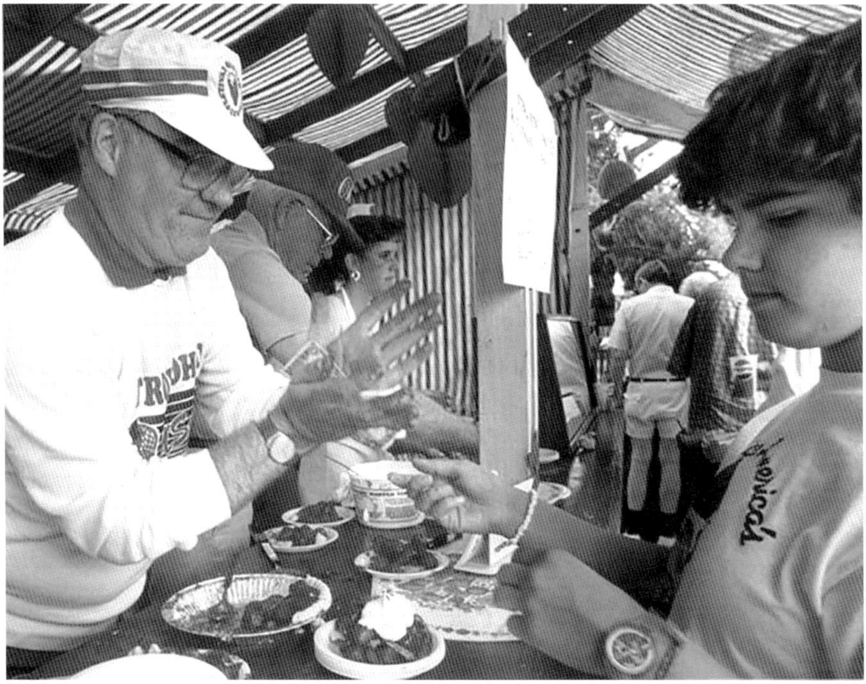

A slice of strawberry pie is sold during the 1988 Troy Strawberry Festival. *Courtesy Ty Greenlees/*Dayton Daily News.

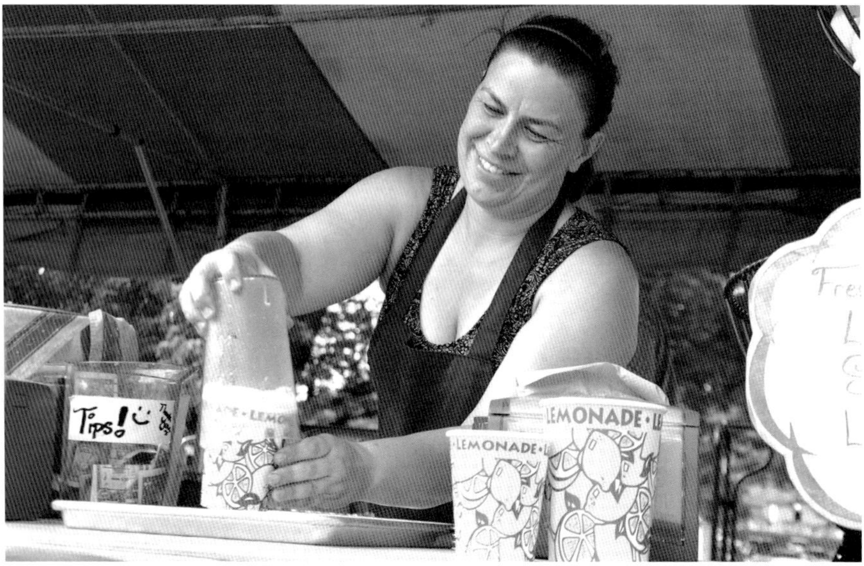

They may not contain strawberries, but lemon shake-ups are a popular beverage at the festival. *Courtesy of the* Troy Daily News.

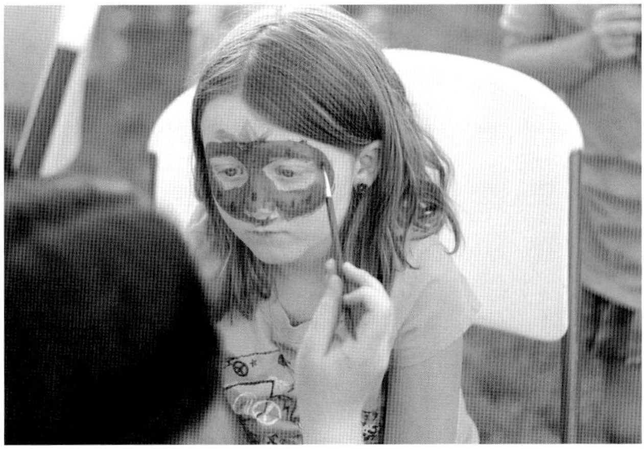

A girl gets her face painted during the Strawberry Festival. *Courtesy of the* Troy Daily News.

"It was by far the largest crowd we've ever had," Beamish said in an interview with the *Troy Daily News*. "Everybody I talked to said it was record-breaking."

The festival definitely benefited from the weather, as temperatures stayed in the seventies most of the weekend.

1989

One year after perfect weather created record crowds, thunderstorms returned again. As is always the case, however, the festival organizers soldiered on through the festival.

"Before the rains, the levee was wall-to-wall people," festival chairman Tim Fourman said in an interview with the *Troy Daily News*. "It was a successful festival, everyone was selling big. As soon as it quit raining, people came back and the crowd grew again. It is that festival spirit."

Chapter 7

IT'S TIME TO MAKE THE DONUTS

From shortcake to cannoli and everything in between, strawberries have found their way into just about every food and beverage served over the forty-plus years of the Troy Strawberry Festival.

There have been strawberry milkshakes, strawberry burritos, strawberry bratwurst, strawberry ice cream, strawberry pies and strawberry salsa, just to name a few. Of course, there are non-strawberry foods as well, just in case someone wants to switch things up. There are giant pork tenderloin sandwiches as big as home plate on a baseball field, thick-cut pork chop sandwiches and fresh-roasted ears of corn on the cob, slathered in buttery goodness.

Over the years, many have tried to eat their way from one side of the Great Miami River levee to the other, only to find at the end their wallets are lighter and their bodies most certainly are not.

For all the food—many of which have contained strawberries, many of which have not—that has been served up in all conceivable ways, however, there is one food that has been served at the Troy Strawberry Festival that reigns supreme.

The Troy Music Boosters' strawberry donuts are the undisputed champions of a festival that is a foodie's delight.

The thick, cake-like strawberry donuts are sold by the dozens during every festival. And by dozens, that means thousands of dozens. Some will line up for hours to get the strawberry donuts fresh out of the fryer, dripping with luscious glaze. Many will walk away with bags filled with dozens to take back with friends and family.

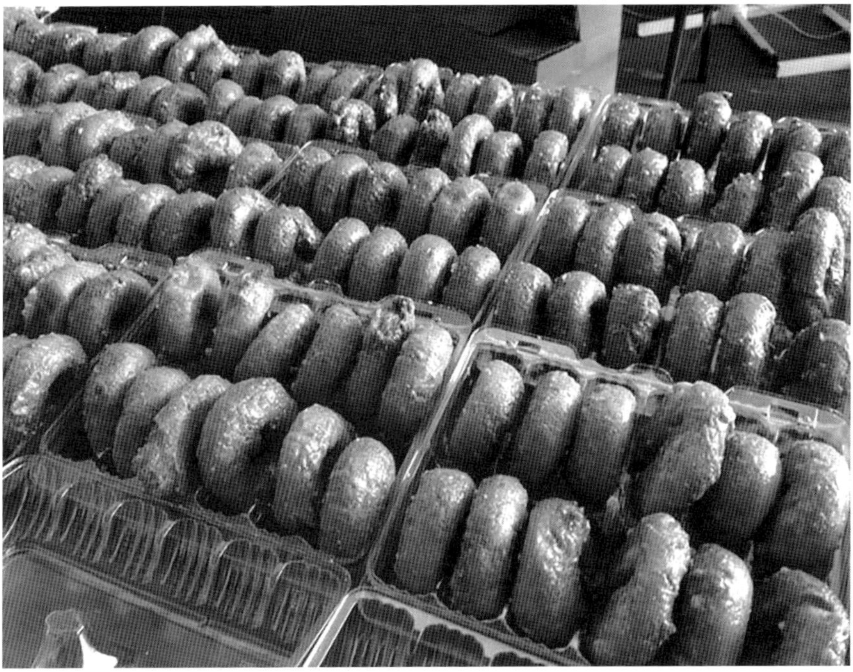

Strawberry donuts are the most popular attraction sold at the Troy Strawberry Festival. *Courtesy Amelia Robinson/*Dayton Daily News.

Some have been known to freeze a few dozen so that they may be enjoyed throughout the year, as the Strawberry Festival that first weekend in June is typically the only time and place they can be purchased. There have been tales of donuts appearing at weddings and donuts being shipped across the country to displaced Trojans.

For some perspective: in a typical year, the Troy Music Boosters, the group that makes and sells the donuts every year, sells about 16,000 (yes, 16,000) dozen donuts at the Troy Strawberry Festival. That's 192,000 donuts. The average donut has about 195 calories, meaning the music boosters are serving up about 37 million calories (37,440,000 to be exact) in donuts every year. A 180-pound person burns up in the neighborhood of 100 calories per mile walked. A person that size would have to walk 374,400 miles to burn off that many delicious donuts. That's a little more than 15 laps around the Earth at the equator.

Have we mentioned how much people love these donuts?

"We have had many companies consistently order large quantities for their employees, or many times, the employees get together and order a large amount and then we deliver to them," said Troy High School band director and Troy City Schools music program director Kathy McIntosh, who has both made the donuts as a student and has overseen the production of millions of donuts as head of Troy's music programs. "The 'Tour de Donut' bike race folks have handed out a donut to participants at the end of the race. People have ordered donuts to have at their wedding receptions. Lots of people freeze them. We recommend freezing them individually, and some people make them last all year.

"We have taken donuts with us to London [England] and given them to the parade sponsors. I have sent the ingredients to Iraq for a graduated band student who was serving during the Gulf War. I have sent them to people from all over the United States who had lived in Troy and moved or friends who just wanted to see what all of the excitement was about."

There is not a musician who has come through Troy in the past forty years who hasn't had some sort of experience making donuts at the Strawberry Festival.

"I worked in the donut booth for the Music Boosters when it was on the levee," Troy High School graduate Stephanie Watern said. "Under a giant tent. Going into my senior year, my parents worked the overnight shift, came home, showered and came to watch me march in the parade with the THS band, and then I went home and changed and went to work the afternoon shift. And boy was it hot. Took what seemed like forever to get the smell of batter out of my clothes. I had learned by then to wear old clothes and shoes. Some years it seemed like you wore more of the batter or icing than was used. It was hot and sweaty work, but in the end, it was worth it."

What has grown into a weekend empire actually had humble beginnings, and in fact, the first year the donuts were served remains largely lost to history. All that's known for sure is the Troy Music Boosters started selling them in the early 1980s, shortly after the first festival in 1977.

"We think 1980," McIntosh said. "John Permenter and possibly Earl Burley were looking for something to sell for the Troy Music Boosters. One of them happened to attend a festival in Port Jefferson where they were making donuts. They inquired, and we rented machines and purchased ingredients from HODCO [Hole In One Donut Company] up until the early 2000s, when the boosters finally bought their own fryers."

Donna McBeath has fond memories of those early days making the donuts. "My mom and dad came out to show us how to run the machines," she said. "The restaurant I worked at in high school bought a machine and started making them. He started selling the machines. I called him to see if we could rent a couple for the weekend. He gave me the name of a dealer in Columbus to contact. My parents came, and we had fifty-pound bags of mix delivered to our house. These had to be separated into individual batches. [Former Troy High School band director] John Slonaker told us it was the only moneymaker they needed. Lots of good memories of so many great band parents."

The donuts are currently made every year in the Troy Memorial Stadium concession stands, which sit next to the Great Miami River levee. This gives the boosters a little bit of distance from the festival, allowing more room for the long lines that generally form to buy the donuts.

In the early days, however, the donuts were made in a tent on the levee, which often led to logjams of donut buyers mixing with people just trying to navigate an already crowded levee. Also, the band sold a variety of donuts those first few years, including strawberry, vanilla and chocolate, which further slowed down the process.

"I have memories of making donuts on the levee, where we originally had a booth," McIntosh said. "There was no tent. The machines were automatic but jammed up frequently. We hand-iced every donut in little tubs. We had three flavors of donuts and three flavors of icing, so you can imagine the amount of time to order and make these. I think that originally made for the long lines. Sure, they were good, but I think people just stood in line because it must be good if the line is long. I doubt if there were a large number of donuts sold in those days because of so many choices."

While it may not have been the most efficient donut-making process, it still brought in plenty of money for the boosters. At one festival, a storm rolled in, and one Troy band parent got left holding the bag—literally.

"The Troy Band parents originally started making and selling the donuts under tents up on the levee," said former Troy resident Carla Lohrer, whose husband, Bill, was a longtime Troy city councilman and grand marshal of the 2008 Troy Strawberry Festival Parade. "One of the years in the early '80s, a very bad storm came through. They said it was a tornado warning, and they came running around telling us to take cover.

"Well, everyone working selling the donuts took off their aprons full of money and shoved them at me. There I stood holding all this money. What to do? I started running with all these money-filled bags and went over the hillside, laid the bags down and laid on top of them. Fortunately, a Troy policeman saw me and came to my rescue. I told him that I had all these bags of money under me. He helped me up, and we ran to his police car, where he put me in the back seat, bags and all. Scary at the time, but funny to think of the experience now."

Over the years, the Troy Music Boosters would continue to streamline the donut-making process. Eventually, the band stopped making different varieties of donuts and settled on what it has become so well known for over the years: the strawberry donut. That, along with the band purchasing its own fryers, turned out to be a game-changer in the Troy Music Boosters' donut empire.

"I'm not sure when it flipped to one kind of donut [sometime between 1983 and 1988], but I think that was monumental," McIntosh said. "This helped to move along the line and the production. When the boosters bought their own fryers, a couple of music booster engineers also created the lean machine that we currently have. Therefore, one type of donut, a specific layout of equipment to maximize efficiency, shift leaders, etc. We have tweaked the production every year, but most of the changes happened in the early 2000s. With this, our production also went up. Before the new fryers, we were lucky to sell eight thousand or so dozen. We have now doubled that production."

The increased production has led to a need for increased donut-making shifts. All members of the Troy music program and their families are expected to volunteer for the process. It's truly a marvel to behold, as the donuts are made in shifts that cover twenty-four hours a day, every day of the festival.

"They work four-hour shifts," McIntosh said. "We have experimented with other lengths, but there is something to be said for practice, and four hours seems to work. By the time the shift is finished, they are cranking them out. We typically start setting up the booth the weekend before the festival. This requires three nights of setting up. We have to remove all of the items from the current concession stand—large/heavy tables, drink coolers, appliances, etc.—sweep/mop/clean the floor, install a double layer of plastic on the floor, covered by three to four layers of cardboard. Cleaning, washing and sanitizing all of the equipment, maintenance on the mixers (we own three old Hobart twenty-quart mixers) and setting up all of the equipment in a specific layout.

"On Tuesday, the ingredients arrive. There are typically fifty to sixty bags of fifty-pound donut mix alone! The grease comes in fifty-pound blocks, again typically around fifty, that we unload outside of the concession stand and then move inside for ease. After set-up, we usually start melting grease around 10:00 a.m. on Wednesday so that we can start frying around 2:00 p.m. Each fryer—we have three—takes about three to four boxes of grease to get started. You have to have a certain amount of grease before you turn the fryers on or it won't go well."

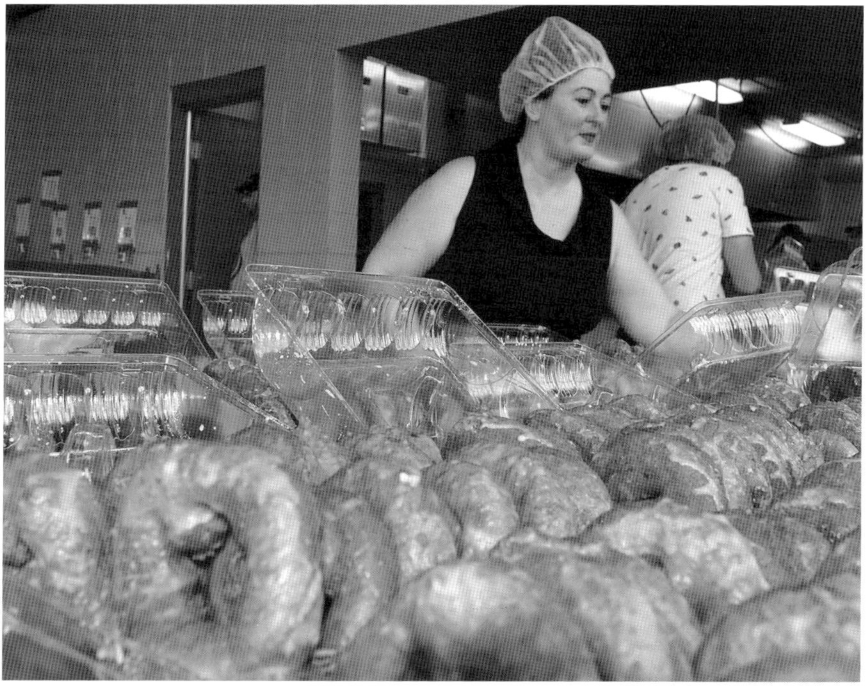

The Troy Music Boosters prepare tens of thousands of strawberry donuts. *Courtesy of the* Troy Daily News.

That's just what it takes to get the donut production facility up and running. The actual making of the donuts is another undertaking all to itself.

"We start frying at 2:00 p.m.., and even though we start then, the best donuts usually start coming out about 6:00 p.m. Wednesday due to the fact that the screens have to re-season and it just takes a while to get good donuts going and won't stop until 6:00 p.m. on Sunday night. We fry 24/7 for those five days. We sell the donuts that we make on Wednesday night the next morning through pre-sales and donut drive-throughs. This continues throughout the weekend. The process goes like this: we mix the donut mix, let it rest for a certain amount of time and load the batter in the dropper bowls; one batch makes about seven drops of between thirty-six to forty donuts each.

"There are two people at the fryer. One drops, both flip. The donuts fry on one side and then are hand-flipped for the other side. The automatic machines do this for you, but also, this is where they *always* jammed up. After they are fried, they drain on a side tray until picked up. Then, the donuts cool on racks. This is important! People always want hot donuts, but if they don't cool, you can't glaze them *and* they become super soggy in the containers. After they have cooled, we glaze—it's a glaze, not an icing. People always complain that they don't have icing, but that isn't what it is supposed to be. Then we put them on a rack to drain and dry.

"They are then put in clear plastic containers that we call clams. We originally used paper donut boxes like you get at the bakery, but they became too soggy. The clams are then placed in plastic bags, three dozen per bag, and stacked in boxes for sale. There are fifty-four dozen in a large box."

Over the years, the donuts have become so popular that an entire mythology has sprung up around them. McIntosh would like to dispel a pair of urban legends that have somehow become apocryphal over the years.

"Urban myth: we do not and have never used cherry flavoring!" McIntosh said. "That rumor got started because the ingredient company accidentally sent a couple of boxes of cherry bits instead of strawberry. They called us and let us know, and we never even let them see the light of day. They have always been strawberry donuts—or vanilla or chocolate in the beginning—NEVER cherry!"

"Urban myth no. 2: we haven't changed the recipe EVER! It is literally the same recipe that we started with in 1980. However, our entire operation is done with volunteers. This is what makes us unique, and I think we are now one of the very few nonprofit groups at the festival that still makes and sells their own product. Because we use volunteers, not everyone is a professional donut maker. They are handmade with care; they are not perfect."

Once the donuts are made, it's time to start distributing them to the crowds, which also can be tricky at times.

"At the height of the festival, we sell a large box every seven minutes," McIntosh said. "On Sunday morning, we start the world's largest math problem, trying to predict how many more to make to meet the demand. We watch sales, look at ingredients and also production time. Our goal is to sell the last donut at 6:00 p.m.

"It has been more than scary at times to be there when you have to tell people that you don't have any more donuts to sell. We typically ask the police to come to the booth to help control the line. Most people are understandable and leave easily, but it isn't always that way. Also, after the event, I typically get quite a few emails or phone calls asking where our bakery is or when we are open next. I just explain to them that I'm really a band director and I would much rather make music, so we won't be making them again for a year."

By the end of the monumental weekend, every musician is left tired, dirty and smelling of frying grease. But in the end, it is worth it because the money raised from the selling of strawberry donuts provides the music program the opportunities to do things others cannot. The Troy Music Boosters found that out the hard way in 2020, when the COVID-19 global pandemic forced organizers to shut down the Troy Strawberry Festival and, in turn, the strawberry donut sales.

"As we unfortunately found out in 2020, the donut sales are crucial to the music department as a whole," McIntosh said. "Band, choir and orchestra are expensive ventures—new instruments, instrument repair, trailer maintenance, uniforms, truck rentals, drivers for trucks, fuel, etc. There is no way a school can individually fund three successful music programs without the help of a booster group.

"Luckily, we had a rainy-day savings account for this 2020, and our costs were reduced because we aren't traveling as much, etc. However, at the end of the 2020–21 school year, that money will run out. The donut sales fund approximately 90 percent of our budgets for the year for all three organizations. In addition, the sales have allowed us to save money for large purchases such as uniforms, risers, large instruments, etc."

Like so many nonprofit organizations in Troy, the Troy Music Boosters are hoping to see the festival return to normal as soon as possible.

So, too, are the thousands who line up every year to purchase a small, round donut that has become a Troy Strawberry Festival tradition and part of the backbone of the Troy High School music program.

Chapter 8

INTO THE 1990s (1990–94)

1990

It rained on Troy's parade.

For the first time in the eleven-year history of the parade, rain was a factor in the 1990 Troy Strawberry Festival Parade. The rains started shortly after the parade began at 9:30 a.m. and continued to fall, heavily at times, for most of the two-hour, two-hundred-unit parade.

Still, though, parade attendees did not let a little precipitation ruin their experience.

"The rain did not appear to dampen anyone's enthusiasm at all," festival chairman Dan Plow told the *Troy Daily News*. "When the rains came down, it was like a sea of umbrellas, but the levee was still packed. That speaks well for the participants and spectators."

The rains would continue throughout the day Saturday, shortening the concert that night at Troy Memorial Stadium, at which the '50s–'60s tribute band Sh-Boom performed.

That year also marked the first year Friday night became a kickoff event for the festival. The Friday Night Kickoff would remain a festival tradition through the present. Typical Friday activities would eventually include the much-loved bed races and the tradition of dyeing the fountain in downtown Troy red for the weekend.

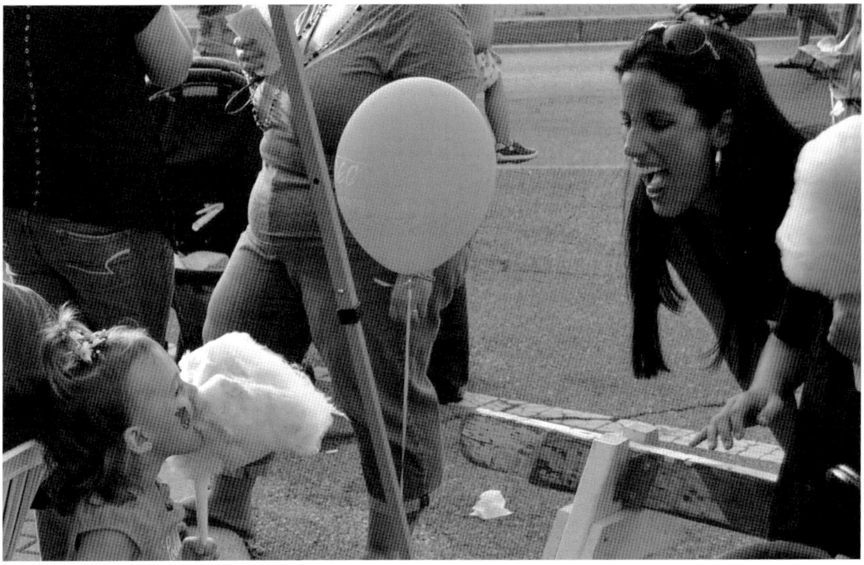

A little girl takes a bite of cotton candy at the Strawberry Festival. *Courtesy of the Karnehm family.*

1991

This was the year the Troy Strawberry Festival went international. Fifteen visitors from Takahashi City, Japan—Troy's sister city—made their inaugural trip to the festival. Troy and Takahashi City first became sister cities in 1989. The following year, then-mayor Douglas Campbell led a group of twelve city delegates on a visit to Japan.

In 1991, a group of Japanese visitors arrived in Troy just in time to visit the Strawberry Festival.

"We are happy to join the Strawberry Festival this year and hope our friendship will deepen further understanding," Japanese representative Takeshi Nakamura told the *Troy Daily News*. "The Strawberry Festival will be one of our best memories of Troy life."

Heavy rains cut the festival a little short on the final day, but otherwise, the festival was deemed a success.

"It went really smooth," chairperson Dee Morton said. "The committee pulled together and everything worked."

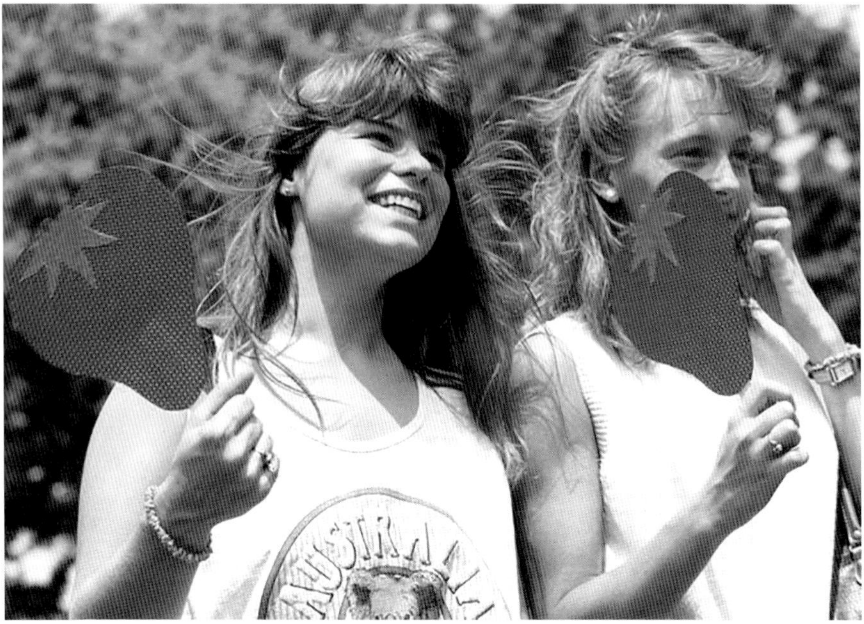

A pair of festivalgoers use strawberry fans to cool off at the Strawberry Festival in 1991. *Courtesy Jan Underwood/*Dayton Daily News.

1992

Bringing more than 150,000 visitors to a small section of a town with a population of a little more than 20,000 has always been a chore for the festival, but things got a little easier in 1992 with the introduction of shuttle buses—provided by the Troy City Schools—which enabled visitors to use a shopping center parking lot on one end of town and take a bus downtown to the festival. The shuttle service would prove to be an invaluable one that would continue to grow and add locations throughout the years.

Those who did take the shuttle to the festival that year likely came home with muddy shoes, as it rained all three days of the festival, including Friday Night Kickoff, featuring the annual bed races. Still, though, the rain didn't stop the festivities.

"We had an amazingly steady crowd for all of the rain," festival chairman Rick Riechert said in an interview with the *Troy Daily News*. "I'd never seen a crowd that big."

1993

Sometimes, a little rain at the Troy Strawberry Festival wasn't always a bad thing. In 1993, rain earlier in the week cooled things off for the festival itself, leading to record crowds.

"It looked like it could be a record weekend," festival chairman Jim Hall said in an interview with the *Troy Daily News*. "I thought it just went great. The weather cooperated, even though it was kind of cold Saturday. Evidently it didn't hurt the booths and it seemed like people were buying things from clubs and organizations and the arts and crafts booths."

In the end, festival officials estimated roughly 200,000 people attended the festival over the course of the three days.

"We definitely think we had a record crowd," said Diana Thompson, the festival's publicity chairwoman, in an interview with the *Troy Daily News*. "It was great. Sunday was beautiful."

The 1993 festival also featured the debut of the Strawberry Jam, an event that saw nearly five hundred high school students fill the floor of Hobart Arena for a dance party.

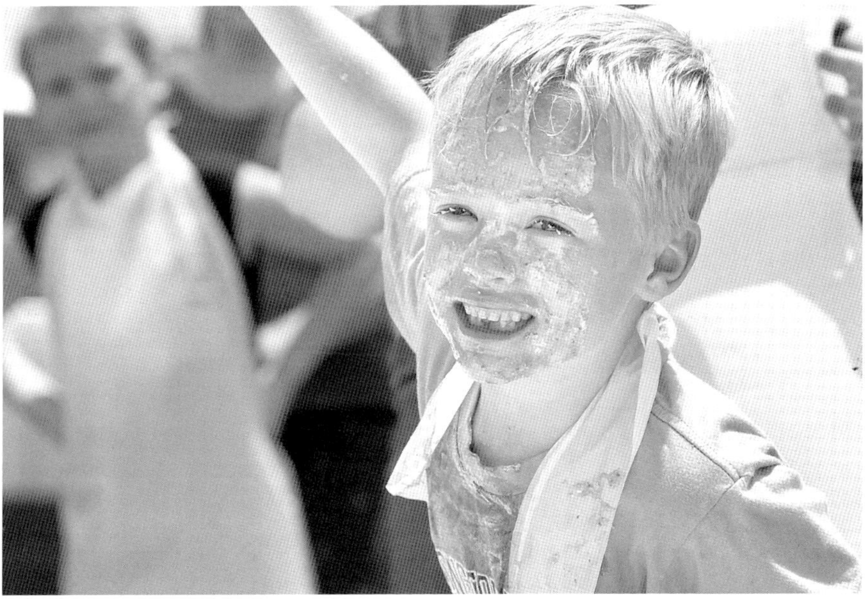

A young boy finishes competing in the pie-eating competition. *Courtesy of the* Troy Daily News.

1994

Perfect skies above led to a packed—and record-setting—levee in 1994.

On Friday night, patrons started lining up at 11:30 p.m. to buy the Troy Band's famous strawberry donuts. That night alone, the band sold more than five hundred dozen of the sweet, doughy concoctions.

On Saturday morning, the levee started filling up with festivalgoers at 9:30 a.m., despite the fact none of the booths opened until 11:00 a.m.

So heavy were the crowds that many booths and vendors reported they had run out of supplies late Saturday afternoon—and either had to close up shop or purchase more supplies for Sunday, the final day of the festival.

"The levee was packed and the bridges had people walking on them all day long," festival chairman Joe Mahan said in an interview with the *Troy Daily News*. "Everybody commented on how smooth everything went. We feel fortunate the weather cooperated throughout the weekend."

Chapter 9

THAT'S ENTERTAINMENT

From the Great Miami River to the levee to Troy Memorial Stadium to downtown Troy and all points in between, Troy has been alive with music.

And clogging.

And ballet.

And frisbee-catching dogs.

Truthfully, when it comes to the Troy Strawberry Festival, practically nothing is off-limits. Since 1977, the Troy Strawberry Festival has done its best not only to bring in regional and national talent but also to serve as a showcase for local performers.

"Entertainment is very important to the festival," current Troy Strawberry Festival manager Kathi Roetter said. "Probably now more than ever, it's important to the festival, especially in terms of bringing in the next generation. The younger people we have coming to the festival want an experience. The things we did to bring in their parents and their grandparents don't necessarily work anymore."

One of the advantages the Strawberry Festival has always had is its location. The festival sits directly in between the Great Miami River and Troy Memorial Stadium, both of which have been heavily used for entertainment purposes over the years. In the early years, the river was used heavily, hosting water skiing and hovercraft demonstrations.

The stadium has hosted many larger concerts over the years, including The Turtles, Paul Revere and the Raiders, McGuffy Lane, The Kentucky Headhunters and several big-name tribute bands.

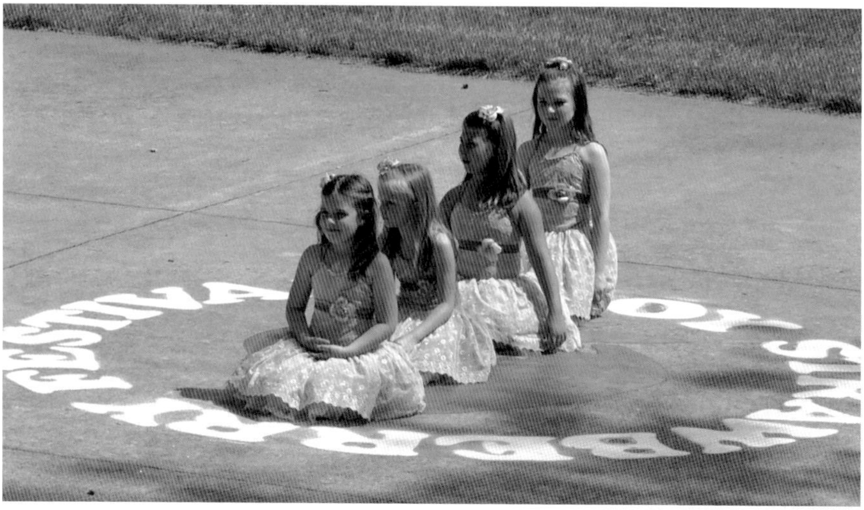

Dancers wait to perform at the Troy Strawberry Festival. *Courtesy of the Karnehm family.*

"Sometime in the 1990s to 2000s, I remember the 1960s band Paul Revere and the Raiders, as well as Flo and Eddie from the Turtles, came to Troy one Saturday evening during the Strawberry Festival," Michael Gwisdala said. "I saw them up close and was too flabbergasted to say anything. I still have their CD I bought from them."

In addition to the stadium and the river, the Troy Strawberry Festival also has the levee, which allows for several smaller stages to be set up. These smaller stages have featured dozens of local acts over the years. When downtown Troy became a permanent part of the festival in 2014, it added yet another venue for entertainers to perform.

"The festival really is in the perfect location," said Kay Hamilton, who served as the festival manager for a number of years. Also, her husband, Steve, was the first festival chairman and is generally regarded as the "father" of the Troy Strawberry Festival. "You have the river right there. You have the stadium right there. You have the levee. It is the perfect place to have a festival. I think that has really helped the festival over the years, having it so centrally located and being able to use all of those things."

One of the most popular acts to perform at the Troy Strawberry Festival was Zoso, a Led Zeppelin tribute band. In addition to putting on a well-received show, their performance led to a funny memory for one local resident.

"I was one of the many sign language interpreters who volunteered to interpret the musical events," Maty Ann Fraley said. "I was a seasoned interpreter; however, signing music really wasn't my strong suit. Many of the other interpreters were much better at signing music than me, but I considered it a challenge and enjoyed it a lot. One year, the big musical entertainment was a Led Zeppelin cover band. I was very excited to do that concert because Led Zeppelin was one of my favorite bands and I knew most of the lyrics. As an interpreter, my job is to interpret the meaning of the words. I was mortified when I got up on the stage and realized, even though I knew the words, most of the meanings escaped me and the other interpreters had to take over for me. I couldn't even fake it like I did with some of the head banging groups that performed. After that, I decided that I would only interpret things that were spoken, not sung."

One popular local band that has performed at the festival year after year was Rum River Blend. "Rum River Blend arrived from California to Troy in 2000 as a duo, composed of myself and Chris Tatarian," Rum River Blend member Linda Tartarian said. "We started playing for the Strawberry Festival that year and were thrilled to participate in the Friday night activities…music on Prouty Plaza, opening ceremonies and the bed races. That tradition carried on for a number of years. The best part about Friday night of the festival was the kids. They were always so excited. We would hand out kazoos, and they would play along and dance to the music. Over the years, we handed out over ten thousand kazoos in the Miami Valley!

"We felt very connected to the festival and played every year until 2015. Over the years, the band grew from two to five players: Linda and Chris

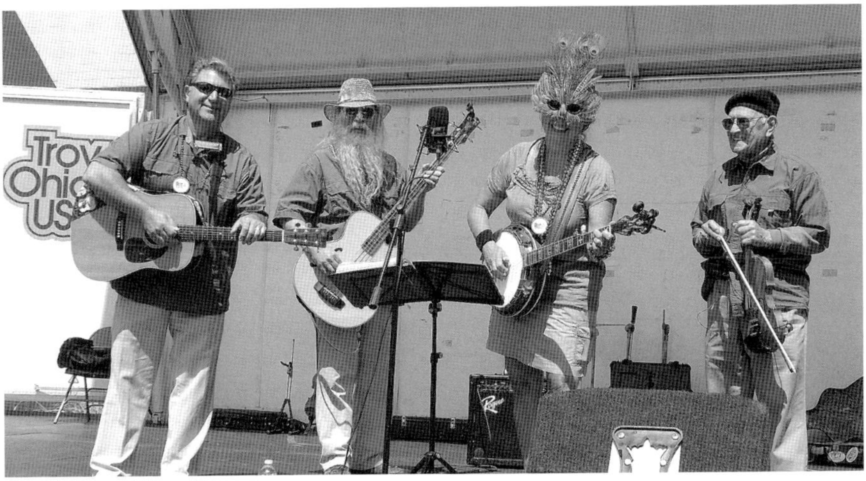

Rum River Blend prepares to perform at the Troy Strawberry Festival. *Courtesy of Linda Tartarian.*

Tatarian, Mark Action, Carl Phillis and Smilin' Bill Benning. It was always an honor to play, and we always looked forward to it.

"We participated in the parade for a number of years, always impressed with the size of the crowds on both sides of the street the entire length of the parade. We loved decorating a trailer, or our truck, or whatever we had that year. We would try to acknowledge the theme of the year. The Strawberry Festival committee was always very welcoming and excited to see us. The crowds gave us all the energy any band could ask for. They were engaged and there for the fun. The best part of playing for the Strawberry Festival was all the food vendors and crafts after we played or going to the Senior Center for strawberry shortcake!"

The festival has also afforded local residents who have lived in the area their entire lives to perform. Some Trojans have performed in multiple entertainment endeavors—some stretching across a broad spectrum of entertainment—over the years.

"I got the privilege of breaking boards with my karate class at the festival, as well as playing with my metal band while I was in high school, too," Troy resident Ben Grilliot said. "Going from that to seeing my kids be involved in the kids' events has been awesome."

Some Troy residents have chosen to stick to more traditional forms of entertainment over the years. "I can remember being in Sing Out Troy and performing at the festival," Yonnie Travis said.

Over the years, performing at the festival has provided fond childhood memories for many who have performed. "I loved getting up early and getting all dressed up in my dance costumes and being in the parade and then going over to the spot and dancing our routines and changing costumes in the tent next to the Troy Senior Citizens Center," Ashley Nadolny said.

Of course, for some, the performances don't end with childhood. In fact, some even continue into their golden years.

"The senior center line dance group performed for the first time in 2019," Claudia Freed Schertzinger said. "A lot of people were surprised that old ladies could dance like that to popular music. We performed at the senior center while people were eating strawberry shortcakes. People were surprised and joined in either singing along or dancing. It was an uplifting experience."

That same year, the dancers from the senior center were able to join another dance group there to entertain festival attendees.

"The seniors line dance group danced with the belly dancers last year," Karen Russell said. "That was an interesting contrast. The belly dancers had a hard time keeping up with us seniors."

Chapter 10

CLOSING OUT THE 1990s (1995–99)

1995

The Best Damn Band in the Land (TBDBITL) was the highlight of what many in southwest Ohio and beyond consider The Best Damn Festival in the Land. The Ohio State University Marching Band not only performed in the Strawberry Festival Parade but also at the festival itself.

Having such a big attraction for the parade that year helped overall attendance at the festival, which had to have some events canceled or cut short because of rain.

"The parade is really what brings the crowd to the festival," festival chairman Bill Myers said in an interview with the *Troy Daily News*. "Usually if the weather is nice, the people at the parade will go over to the festival. I think we are semi-related to the weather."

1996

Fireworks lit up the skies above as the Troy Strawberry Festival celebrated twenty years with a "Berried Treasure" theme.

"When I got here today, I couldn't believe the size of the crowd," festival chairwoman Diana Thompson said in an interview with the *Troy Daily News*. "It's been a glorious day and that's helped get the people out. I have a lot of people to thank when this is over. All of these volunteers are working until they are ready to drop to make the festival successful."

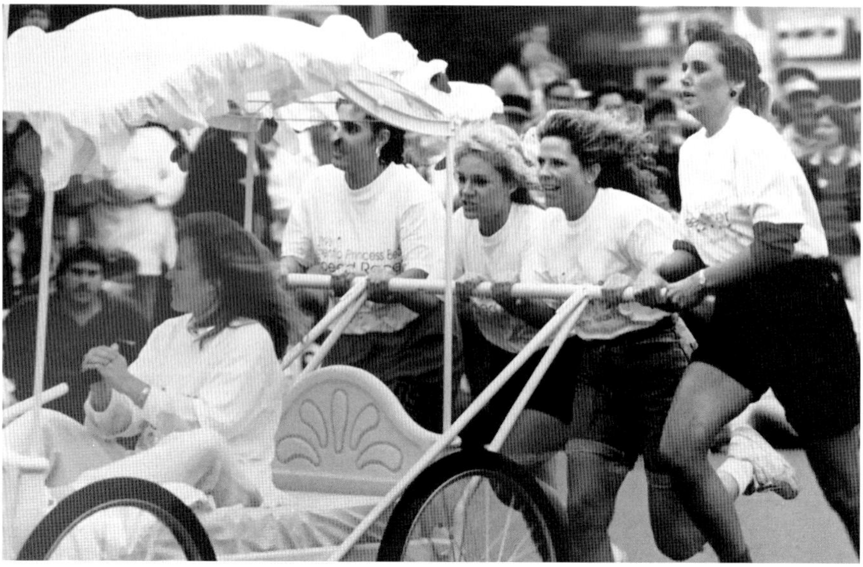

The Evenflo team competes in the 1993 bed races. *Courtesy of Martha Herrick Bravo.*

1997

The traditional Christmas tree went up in the center of town, wreaths dotted the levee and Christmas lights lit up the night as Troy celebrated the 1997 festival with a "Berry Christmas" theme.

"Everything went like clockwork," festival chairman Chuck Lobaugh said in an interview with the *Troy Daily News*. "We had huge crowds both days, despite the cloudy weather. Everything went great. We had no problems. We had a wonderful, terrific, fantastic festival."

The 1997 festival also featured another concert in Troy Memorial Stadium, this time by country music star Kevin Sharp, who sang his hit song "Nobody Knows."

1998

There was a little bit of everything—including unseasonably cool temperatures for the first week of June—at the 1998 Troy Strawberry Festival.

The cool temperatures helped bring out more strawberry enthusiasts, as chairman Tom Kendall and the rest of the festival officials estimated it was one of the biggest crowds in festival history.

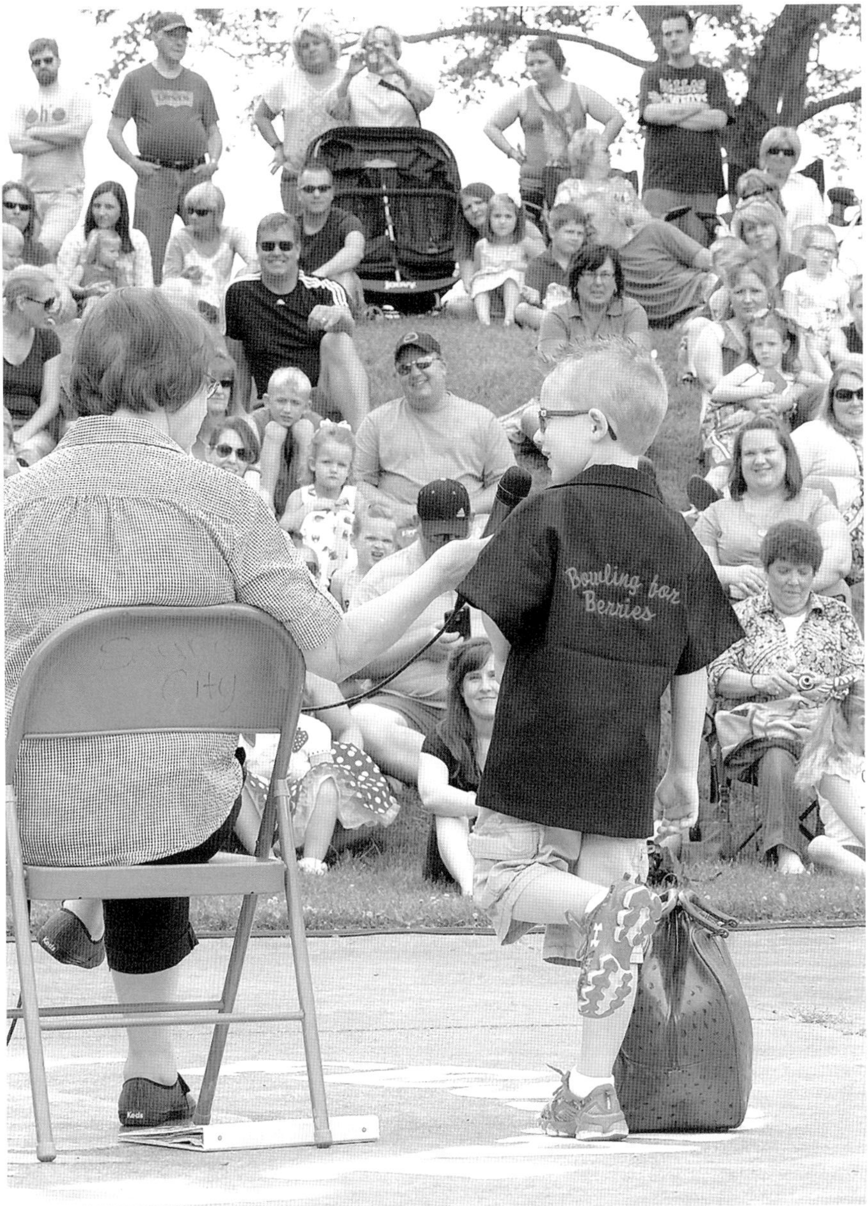

A young boy participates in the Little Mister Strawberry competition. *Courtesy of the* Troy Daily News.

Once again, visitors from Takahashi City were in attendance for the festival.

The highlight of the weekend was another concert at Troy Memorial Stadium, this one featuring 1960s rock-and-roll legends The Turtles and Paul Revere and the Raiders.

1999

One year after one of the coolest festivals in history, the twenty-third annual Troy Strawberry Festival proved to be one of the warmest, with temperatures soaring into the nineties, keeping the numbers down over some previous years.

"If you can't stand the heat, don't come out here," festival chairman Jody Davis told the *Troy Daily News*. "We don't want anyone to get hurt out here."

Over the festival's many years, the Great Miami River was used on and off for various events, from "river rat regattas" to water skiing shows. The 1999 festival featured a new use, however, as thousands of rubber ducks were poured into the river off the Adams Street Bridge. The numbered ducks all were purchased by contestants as part of a festival fundraiser. The ducks could win prizes for their "owners," based on their finish, with the grand prize being a brand-new pickup truck.

Chapter 11

GETTING COMPETITIVE

The Troy Strawberry Festival has always been a family-style event meant to bring the city together. Sometimes, however, when family gets together, competition breaks out.

Since its inception, competitions have been a key part of the Troy Strawberry Festival. Some events have practically become synonymous with the festival. Others have come and gone. Some have gone away, then come back again, depending on their popularity and participation.

There's seemingly some sort of competition for just about every age and skill level. Whether you are a high-level runner or cyclist or can just eat strawberry pie at an incredible rate of speed, there's a Troy Strawberry Festival competition out there waiting for you.

In addition to providing all manner of ribbons, trophies and medals, however, the Troy Strawberry Festival has, more than anything else, provided memories for all of its participants. Whether finishing in first place or coming in dead last, there's been no shortage of smiles over the years.

Here's a look at some of the many events that have been a part of the festival—some of which have been there for decades and some of which have come and gone in a flash.

Strawberry Festival Soccer Invitational

It started out as a dream.

More than two decades ago, longtime Troy soccer coach and enthusiast John Permenter wanted to put together a youth soccer tournament for teams in the region. In 2018, the Troy Strawberry Soccer Invitational celebrated its twentieth tournament with games on Saturday and Sunday in Troy, Piqua and Tipp City.

"It's a magic moment," Dave Pappas, who co-chairs the event along with his wife, Becky, said in an interview with the *Troy Daily News*. The husband-and-wife team have been part of the tournament from its inception, first coaching their children's teams before eventually joining the group of dedicated volunteers who help make the event happen every year.

Of all the competitive events that take place as part of the Strawberry Festival, the Strawberry Soccer Invitational is by far the biggest.

Permenter—who passed away in 2013—was able to see the tournament he helped create grow into one of the largest in the Midwest. When the tournament was first held in 1998, it took place at a single location, Duke Park in Troy. The tournament has long since outgrown Duke and takes place at five locations: Duke Park, Archer Park and Ferguson Field in Troy, Pitsenbarger Park in Piqua and Kyle Park in Tipp City.

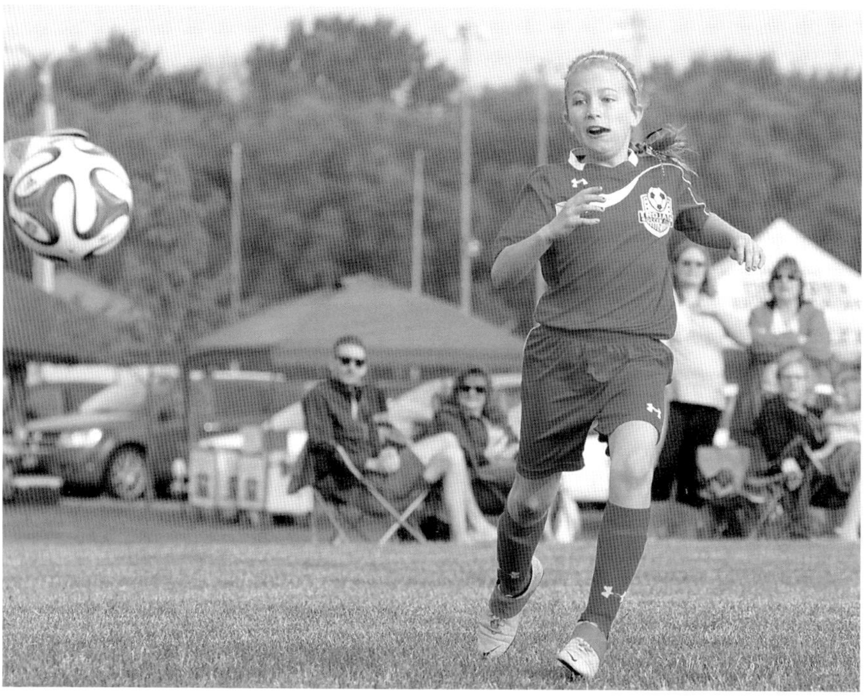

Kara Steinke chases after the ball during the Troy Strawberry Festival Class Soccer Invitational. *Courtesy of the* Troy Daily News.

Also, the tournament used to be held during Strawberry Festival weekend in Troy, hence its name. Eventually, however, the tournament outgrew the first weekend in June and tournament organizers found it too hard to find enough volunteers split between the soccer tournament and the Strawberry Festival itself.

Money raised from the event through entry fees, parking, concessions and souvenir sales goes to benefit youth soccer programs in all four of the host communities.

"No, not at all," Pappas said when asked if he ever thought the tournament would grow as big as it has. "Especially in terms of the size. I think it was always our vision that it would continue as long as it has, but I don't know that we ever thought it would get as big as it has. Youth soccer has continued to grow and we've kind of grown right along with it."

As the tournament has grown and progressed over the years, so have the volunteers running it—to the point Pappas said he feels confident it will be around for the next twenty years and beyond.

"We feel like we've got the depth on our committee and the quality we are looking for," Pappas said.

Super Cities Competition

The Super Cities Competition started out as a way for teams of competitors from Troy and surrounding cities to go head-to-head in what was originally supposed to be a series of lighthearted, fun games intended to entertain an audience as much as anything else.

"When we started, the idea was just for everyone to get together and have some fun," said 1978 Strawberry Festival chairman Doug Trostle, who not only helped come up with the idea for the Super Cities Competition but also was a competitor for a number of years. "It was based off a game show at the time called *Almost Anything Goes*, which had all kinds of wacky-type stunts that people would do in order to win prizes. And that's really what we were trying to do. In order to keep things even, every team had to have a certain number of males, a certain number of females, competitors in certain age groups and that sort of thing.

"When it started out, it really was just meant to be a fun competition between the teams from different cities. What we found out pretty quickly, though, is just how competitive it would get. People really started taking it seriously pretty fast."

The first-ever Super Cities Competition in 1978 featured the following events:

- The Sock Hop: A sack race that started with two team members and then added contestants until each team had to cross the finish line with five team members sharing the same burlap sack.
- Paramedic Pastime: Teams had to transport a beach ball on a stretcher through an obstacle course without letting the ball fall at any time.
- Strawberry Shuffle: A leapfrog competition across the football field inside Troy Memorial Stadium.
- Friendly's Fundae Sundae: Inspired by primary host Friendly Ice Cream, the teams had to build a "sundae" around one teammate out of inner tubes. That teammate then had to make his or her way—often waddling—across a finish line.
- Deliver the Mail: Contestants had to put on a coat, hat, scarf, gloves and wading boots, pick up a letter and get pulled in a wagon by other teammates to a golf cart, which was then driven by another teammate to a mailbox, where they had to deliver a letter.
- Chicken and the Egg: A three-legged race in which teammates had to deliver an "egg" (in this case, a Nerf football) from one end of the stadium to the other.
- Mrs. O'Leary's Nightmare: Teams had to form a bucket brigade and deliver water from one large canister to another.
- Maids' Mayhem: Field hockey using brooms and beach balls.
- Jim Dandy: A sundae-eating competition named after one of Friendly Ice Cream's popular ice cream treats.

The first Super Cities Competition featured teams from Troy, Piqua, Tipp City, West Milton, Greenville and Covington. Over the years, some cities were added and some would drop out of the competition.

"We represented the city of Huber Heights in city challenges way back when," Bonnie Miller said. "We had to petition to be included since part of Huber Heights was in Miami County. Had a great time competing and riding a float in the parade. My husband and I grew up in Troy and graduated from THS."

The Super Cities Competition was incredibly popular in the festival's early years, as thousands would show up to watch the competition inside

Troy Memorial Stadium. Eventually, however, it would lose steam over the years, as cities struggled to fill full teams.

The event has been revived several times over the years, but currently there is no Super Cities Competition at the Troy Strawberry Festival.

Super Kids Competition

The Super Kids Competition was a scaled-down version of the Super Cities Competition. Rather than competing as teams, however, kids from around Troy had the opportunity to compete as individuals in different age groups.

Much like the Super Cities Competition, events varied over the years, although they typically included mini-obstacle courses, baseball tosses, sprints and timed sack races.

Looking back on the history of the competition, the winners' list often reads like a who's who of kids who would go on to excel as athletes at Troy High School. Two such athletes were brothers Matt and Chris Jackson; their father, Rick, was the chairman of the 1979 Troy Strawberry Festival. Matt would go on to excel in both football and baseball at Troy High School before moving on to play catcher for the Wooster College baseball team. Younger brother Chris played football and track at Troy and then went on to become an offensive lineman at Ohio University.

Their mother, Susan, who was the Strawberry Festival Parade chairwoman in 1982, remembers one Strawberry Festival Super Kids Competition in particular. "In 1984 or '85, we had stepped away from being so involved with Strawberry Festival, unlike the dedicated souls who worked all year long to make the festival what it has become today," she said. "We had a trailer on Grand Lake and went up there to 'escape' on weekends. Matt and Chris loved the Super Kids Competition and both enjoyed the thrill of winning their age group for several years each.

"This particular year, our plan to get out of Troy on Strawberry Festival weekend was met with tears as both boys were devastated that they wouldn't be there for Super Kids, so we surprised them, took them to the levee for the early morning competition then jumped in the packed car and headed to the lake. Coming back to Troy on Sunday, they insisted that we stop to see if just maybe there was a trophy waiting for them. Of course, we tried to tell them that so many kids participated, yada yada, don't get your hopes up. Happy ending, Matt won his age division (probably nine or ten), Chris also placed (five or six). Yay! More trophies to collect cobwebs on their bedroom shelves!"

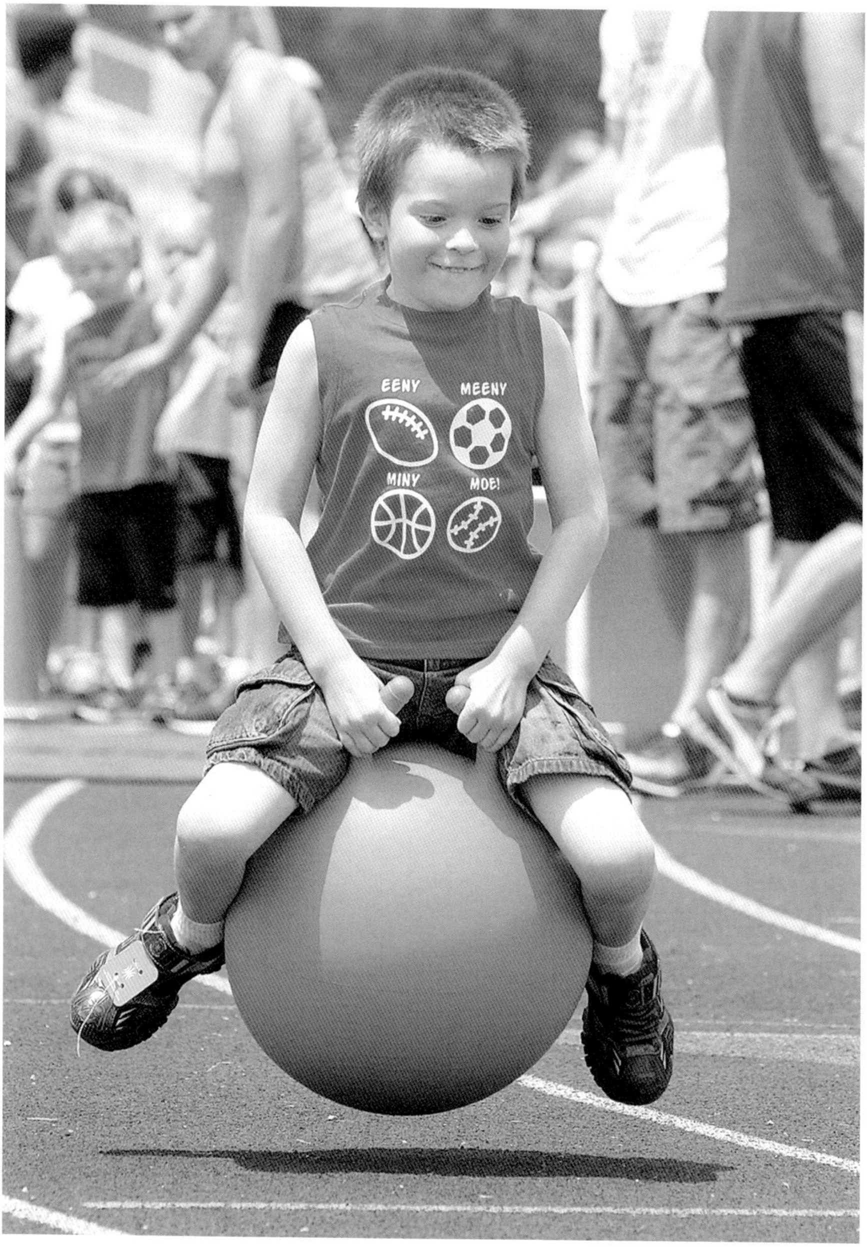

A child bounces on a ball during the Super Kids Competition. *Courtesy of the* Troy Daily News.

Much like the Super Cities Competition, the Super Kids Competition started out hot, with hundreds of children participating every year, but the numbers would eventually start to wane over the years until the competition shut down completely and went away. Since then, the Super Kids Competition has made its return several times but has never managed to get the same foothold it once had.

The Troy Strawberry Festival Junior Golf Tournament

The golf tournament, for boys and girls ages eight to eighteen in appropriate age groups, is held yearly at Troy's Miami Shores Golf Course. The event typically features not only the top high school golfers in the area but also younger golfers who go on to star for their respective high school teams.

Participation in the event has typically seen an ebb and flow that coincides with the sport on a national level. In the late 1990s into the early 2000s, when Tiger Woods was at the height of his popularity and America was experiencing a golf boom, the tournament had its highest participation numbers.

The Troy Strawberry Festival Junior Tennis Tournament

Much like the golf tournament, the tennis tournament is for boys and girls throughout the area and is divided up into age groups. Players can participate in both singles and doubles tournaments.

Also like the Strawberry Festival Junior Golf Tournament, participation levels in the tennis tournament often coincide with the general popularity of the sport in America.

Pickleball

Pickleball is an event that has only recently become a part of Strawberry Festival weekend. It is a paddleball sport that combines elements of badminton, table tennis and tennis. Two or four players use solid paddles made of wood or composite materials to hit a perforated polymer ball with twenty-six to forty round holes over a net.

The sport has caught on in Troy, especially among older players who may no longer be able to play full-court tennis, with games played almost daily at the Miami County YMCA and Duke Park, when the weather allows.

CORNHOLE

Cornhole is another event that has only recently been added to the Troy Strawberry Festival. As the bean bag toss game became increasingly popular, particularly in the Midwest, it became a staple of the Troy Strawberry Festival.

THE TROY VERSUS PIQUA ALUMNI FLAG FOOTBALL GAME

This is an event that actually started out independent of the Troy Strawberry Festival but eventually became incorporated into the festival. Every year since 1899, the Troy High School and Piqua High School football teams

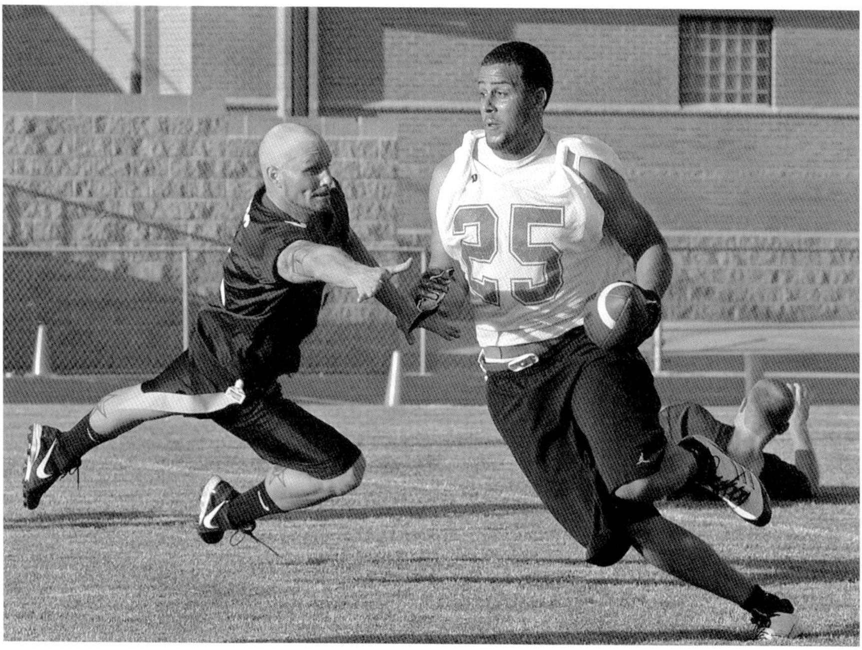

Shane Carter carries the ball for Troy during the annual Troy-Piqua Alumni Flag Football Game. *Courtesy of the* Troy Daily News.

have played each other, making it one of the oldest high school football rivalries not only in the state but also the nation. No two teams in the state of Ohio have played each other more.

Over the years, both teams have experienced tremendous success, as well, becoming two of the winningest programs in the state. The two schools have combined to send hundreds of players on to college football and more than a dozen to the NFL. It's also a hotly contested rivalry, with Troy leading the series by the slimmest of margins, 66-64-6.

The games are always played in front of thousands of fans, with a whopping fourteen thousand shoehorning their way into Troy Memorial Stadium in 1992 to see the two teams plays each other.

With so much at stake and so much hoopla surrounding the game, it's easy to see how playing each other three or four times in a high school career simply isn't enough to get it out of one's system. In 2005, the first Troy versus Piqua Alumni Flag Football Game was played, with proceeds from ticket sales and a silent auction of football memorabilia going to the educational funds at both schools.

The location of the game alternated between Troy and Piqua for four years before the game itself eventually died off. It was eventually brought back and made a key component of the Troy Strawberry Festival's Friday Night Kickoff. The two teams play a flag football game inside Troy Memorial Stadium.

10K Classic Run

The Troy Strawberry Festival Classic typically helps kick off the festival on Saturday with a morning run—perhaps clearing the way for competitors to devour thousands of calories in festival food. The event features age groups from under fourteen all the way to seventy over as hundreds enter the race. It's one of the top 10K races in the area, drawing some of the top runners in southwest Ohio. Of course, it's also an opportunity for less experienced runners to compete.

Miami East football coach Max Current—himself a former high school and college defensive lineman—remembers the time he entered the race on a dare. "I ran the 10k in 1981," Current said. "I finished in 398th place in fifty-three minutes and nineteen seconds. I still have my running number badge. I was talking smack about how good I could do in the race; my dad called my bluff and brought me home an entry form. The most I ever ran

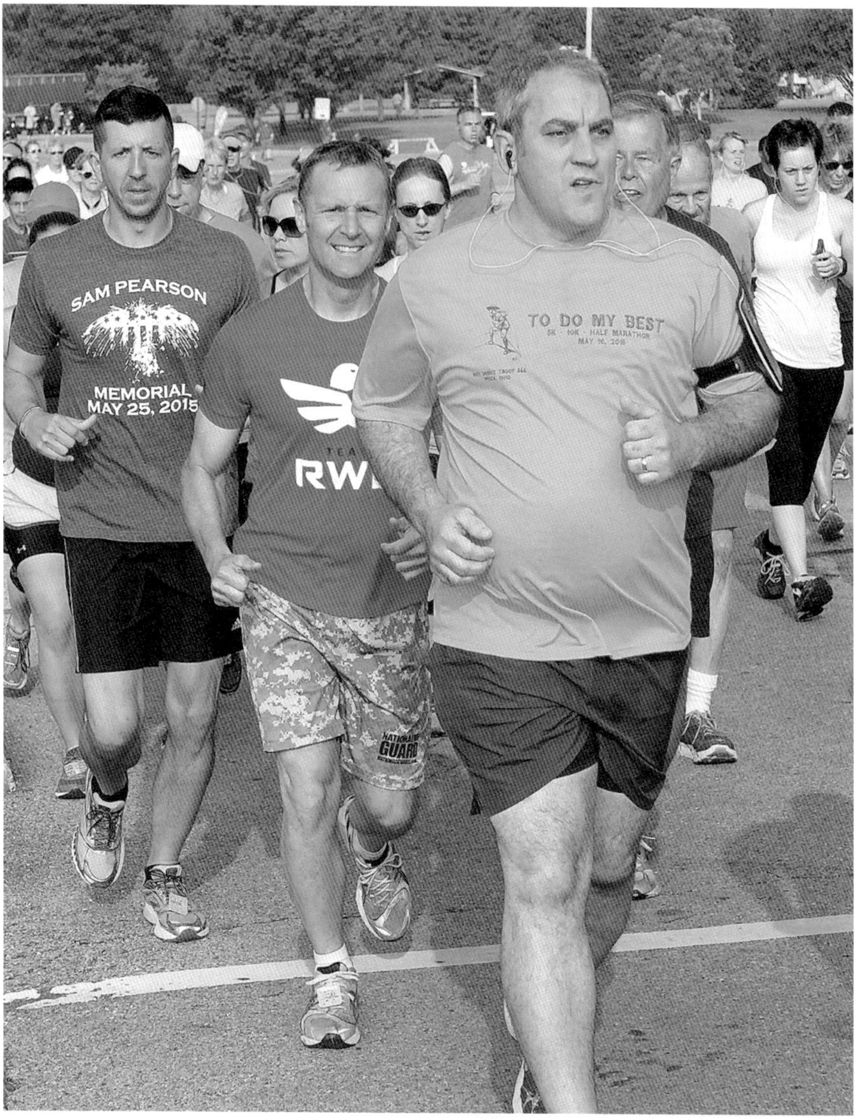

Runners compete in the Troy Strawberry Festival 10K Classic. *Courtesy of the* Troy Daily News.

before was to Casstown from my house, which I did one time, or around the block of 55 to Sayers to Lefevre to Staunton back to State Route 55. I did this one time."

In addition to the 10K race, there's also a yearly 1K Strawberry Shortcake Fun Run for those who aren't quite as competitive.

Bike Time Trials

The bicycle time trials event has seen changes over the years—mostly regarding the distance—but has been a mainstay throughout much of the festival's history.

One year, the event was won by Troy High School Athletic Hall of Fame member Todd Darbyshire. Darbyshire is, without question, the most decorated wrestler in Troy High School history, having won a state championship in the early 1980s. In addition to his wrestling, Darbyshire was known for his incredible fitness levels.

When he went on to wrestle at The Ohio State University, it wasn't all that uncommon for Darbyshire to ride his bike back and forth from Columbus to Troy on the weekends, a distance of roughly eighty miles. On one of those trips home in June, he came home to find out his friends had signed him up for the Strawberry Festival Bike Time Trials—the morning after he had completed the eighty-mile ride home.

"I didn't even have my racing bike with me," Darbyshire said. "I just had my regular bike."

And how did he do?

"I won," he said. "But I probably could have done better."

Softball

A slow-pitch softball tournament has been a Strawberry Festival mainstay for a number of years. With a men's tournament, women's tournament and co-ed tournament, it offers large numbers of players the opportunity to compete during Strawberry Festival weekend.

Pie-Eating Contest

This is an event that is almost as much fun for the spectators as it is for the competitors. The event is as the name would imply—competitors have to eat a strawberry pie as quickly as possible. The event is based on time rather than the number of pies eaten.

There is no pie crust, just a pie tin filled with strawberries, strawberry gel and mounds of whipped cream. The results are always particularly messy. Strawberry Festival officials, including the chairman or chairwoman,

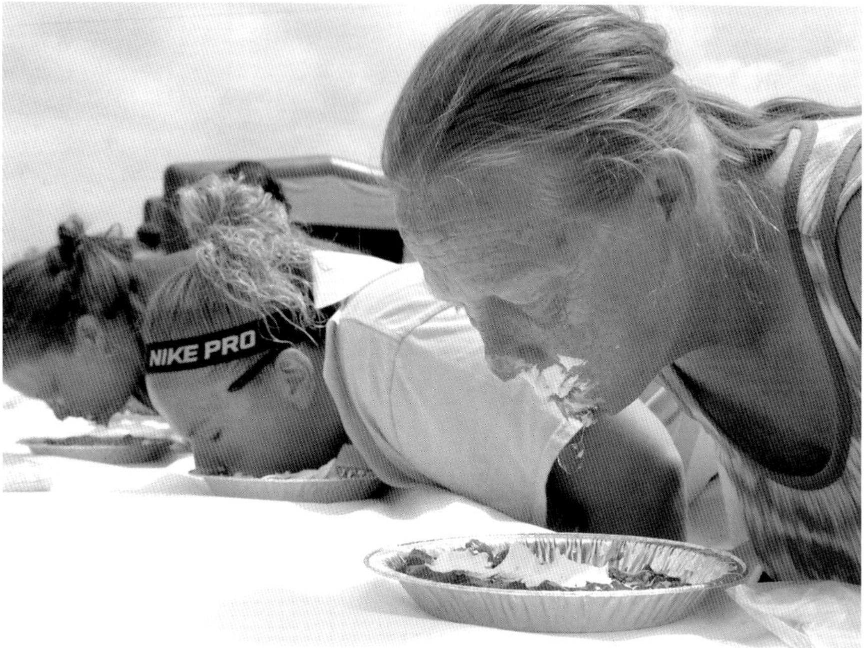

Competitors dive right into the pie-eating contest. *Courtesy of the* Troy Daily News.

typically enter the event—and almost always end up with pies getting smashed in their faces.

In addition to Strawberry Festival dignitaries entering the event, local "celebrities" often enter as well. Former Troy High School principal Bill Overla remembers winning the event in 2014. "I think I finished in 1:30," Overla said. "I had been training for that event my entire life."

Matthew Watkins, the 2018 Troy Strawberry Festival chairman, was the announcer for the event in 2018. He said his favorite part was watching the kids compete. "The adults are a very competitive group, but the kids do this for fun," Watkins said in a *Troy Daily News* interview. "I had a little girl one time who never took a bite. When it was done, she asked for a fork. She played me for a free pie."

Diaper Derby

Very much like the pie eating contest, the Troy Strawberry Festival Diaper Derby is an event that is as much fun, if not more fun, for the spectators as

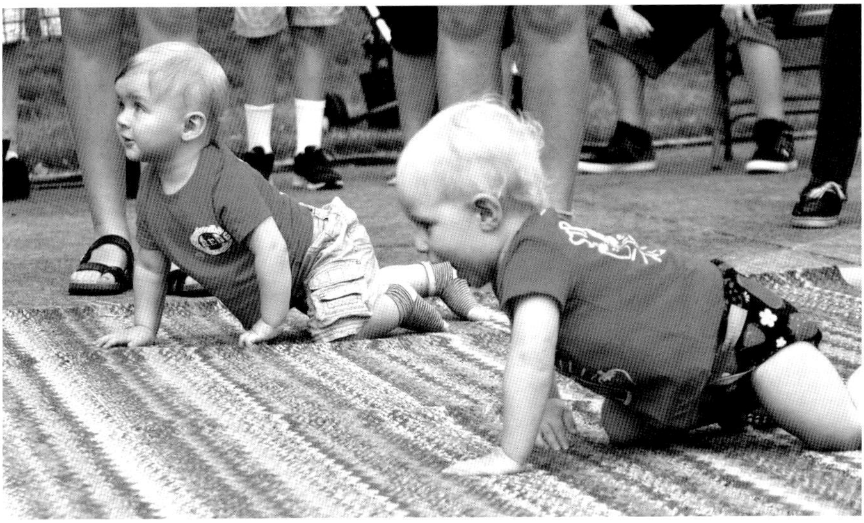

Babies compete in the Diaper Derby. *Courtesy of the* Troy Daily News.

the competitors. In fact, most of the competitors in the Diaper Derby don't even realize they are competing.

In the Diaper Derby, the contestants—all babies who are not yet walking—line up on one end of a carpeted stage with their parents at the other end behind the finish line, trying to encourage their sons or daughters to be the first to crawl across the line for the win.

"Diaper Derby is one of the best events because the babies are so cute and everyone likes the babies and it's funny and it's just a lot of fun," former Strawberry Festival chairwoman Becky Pappas said.

In addition to the race itself, there's also a costume contest for the babies, which is judged by that year's Strawberry Festival queen and her court.

River Races

In the early days of the Troy Strawberry Festival, the Great Miami River played a much larger role than it would in later years, to include several boating demonstrations and water-skiing competitions.

The first Troy Strawberry Festival featured a canoe race, using traditional watercraft.

The second festival, in 1978, featured both a "Poor Man's Regatta" and an "Anything Floats" competition. The rules of Anything Floats were simple: as the name implied, contestants could use anything that floated to navigate their way down the river. "You could race in a rubber inner tube with a paddle and win this race," event organizer Ken Davis said in a 1978 *Troy Daily News* interview.

The Poor Man's Regatta was a shorter race, in which boats were built from nontraditional items such as plastic bottles, empty beer cans (preferably emptied well in advance of the competition), styrofoam, oil drums, sealed cans, inner tubes, old bathtubs, balloons, chicken wire, bubble gum or bobby pins. The seaworthiness of many of these watercrafts were questionable at best, which may explain why they only lasted at the festival for a few years. By the time the mid-1980s had rolled around, the races on the Miami River had become nothing but a memory.

BEACH VOLLEYBALL

For a short while, beach volleyball was a Strawberry Festival competition. Tons of sand were dumped on the floodplain in between the Great Miami River and the levee, allowing beach volleyball competitions.

Ultimately, this competition was largely dependent on the weather, as a few heavy rains would sometimes make the court unplayable. This likely led to the competition's quick departure from the Strawberry Festival lineup.

FIREFIGHTER WATERBALL

Waterball is described as a tug-of-war with water. Two teams of three firefighters compete in each round using a fire hose to blast water at a ball suspended on a long overhead cable. The first team to push the ball over to the opposing team's side wins.

At the Strawberry Festival, local fire departments would compete against one another. This is another event that is no longer part of the festival.

Chapter 12

THE FESTIVAL IN THE NEW MILLENNIUM (2000–05)

2000

The city of Troy celebrated a new millennium with an old tradition: the twenty-fourth annual Troy Strawberry Festival.

"Everything went fantastic," festival chairman Stan Kegley said in an interview with the *Troy Daily News*. "The weather was gorgeous. This was a banner year. I can safely say it was an exceptional crowd."

The 2000 festival also featured the debut of the Kiddie Tractor Pull, in addition to the festival's more traditional big wheel races.

2001

The 2001 Troy Strawberry Festival highlight was a laser-light show in the skies above on the Saturday night of the festival.

Cool, rainy conditions did affect attendance at the festival that year, however, although crowds remained relatively steady.

"The crafts people are doing well," festival chairman Phil Trentine said in an interview with the *Troy Daily News*. "I've been talking to the vendors. Cold foods and drinks are down. Hot foods are up. I try to patrol the levee and see how folks are doing."

2002

Hot temperatures kept the drinks and cool refreshments flowing, but they were not enough to keep the crowds away from the 2002 Strawberry Festival, themed "All Abuzzzzz…About Strawberries."

The theme seemed a perfect fit, as an estimated 105,000 people swarmed to the levee on the first day alone. By the second day, the festival had exceeded 200,000 in attendance.

"The weather was really sweet—we almost had too much sun, though," festival chairwoman Sally Reichert said in an interview with the *Troy Daily News*. "Saturday, groups sold out of items. Our Pepsi vendors had to replenish their trucks, which doesn't usually happen. We went through a lot of soda and water, anything that was a beverage. We had nice, steady crowds. About 200,000 people attended this year."

2003

The 2003 festival featured a unique event: the unveiling of Miami County's Bicentennial Bell, which was part of the state of Ohio's Bicentennial Bell Tour. The specially inscribed bronze bell stands two feet tall and weighs in at about 250 pounds. The casting ceremonies were set to coincide with Troy's annual Strawberry Festival.

"As this bell will be cleaned and polished to reveal a beautiful shine, so too does Miami County shine brightly through the spirit of hard work and dedication of our families, friends and neighbors and the caring spirit that makes us proud to call Miami County our home," Ohio state representative Diana Fessler said as she read a proclamation to the crowd. "When this bell rings proudly for the first time, may its echo reverberate for generations to come as a reminder of our goodly past and precious hard-won liberties."

Heavy storms would bring a premature end to the festival on the final day.

"Even with the weather, I have no negative comments," festival chairwoman Roberta Jacobs said. "Saturday was more than expected. We had so many vendors say that they'd made more Saturday than they'd ever sold. And some had been coming for twenty years. If our clubs and organizations had a good festival, then we were successful. All indications were that they did very good."

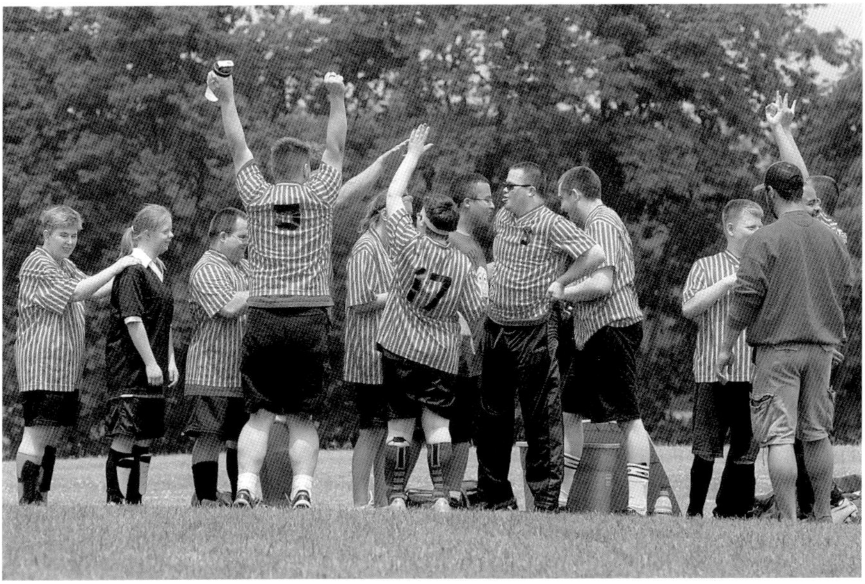

The team from Riverside of Miami County celebrates during the Strawberry Special Olympics. *Courtesy of the* Troy Daily News.

2004

For the first time in five years, the festival caught a break from the weather, as sunny skies and temperatures in the seventies brought out record crowds, making the 2004 theme, "Heavenly Strawberries," seem entirely appropriate.

"This is fantastic. You couldn't ask for anything better," festival chairwoman Susan Fogt said in an interview with the *Troy Daily News*. "It wouldn't be a festival without all the volunteers who put so much effort and dedication into this. Their commitment is incredible. Of course, we have a lot of fun, too."

2005

The twenty-ninth annual Troy Strawberry Festival was highlighted by an appearance from the world-famous Anheuser-Busch Clydesdales as part of the parade. The massive horses were on a tour across the nation as part of their company's Here's to the Heroes Tour 2005. Not only were they part of the parade, but they were housed at the Miami County Fairgrounds in the days leading up to the parade, allowing residents to get an up-close-

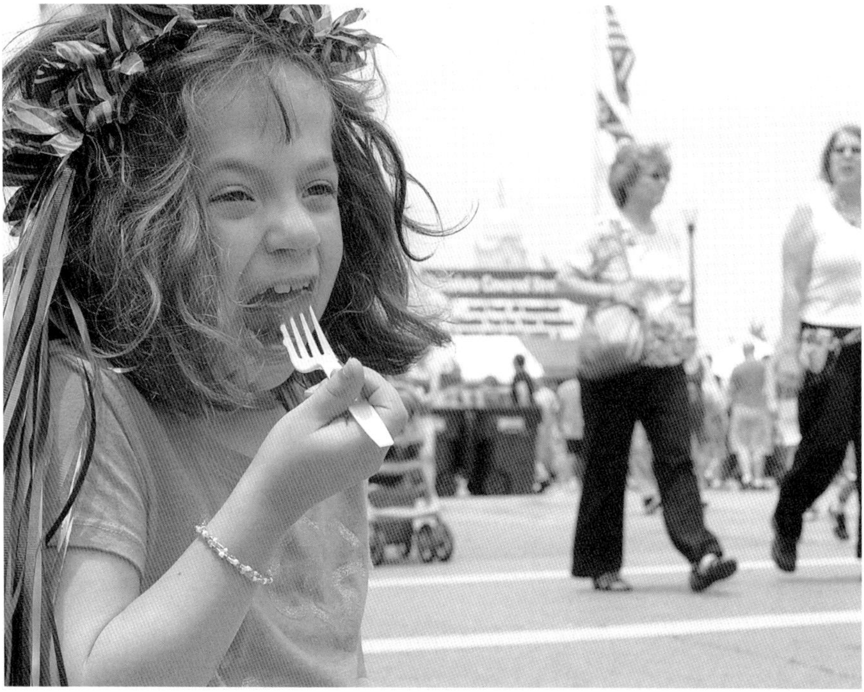

A young girl takes a big bite of a fresh strawberry. *Courtesy of the* Troy Daily News.

and-personal look at the Clydesdales, all of which weighed in somewhere between 1,800 and 2,000 pounds.

The entire tour was a tribute to American military members. "We hope this salute will serve as a small token of our heartfelt appreciation to our nation's military for all the sacrifices they and their families make," August Busch IV, president of Anheuser-Busch, Inc., said in a press release. "It's important for our military to know they have our nation's support. They fight for our freedom we enjoy every day and we should never take that freedom or our American way of life for granted."

One of the highlights at the festival was the Troy-Piqua Alumni Flag Football Game, featuring teams of former Troy and Piqua football players competing against one another inside Troy Memorial Stadium. Troy versus Piqua is the most-played high school football rivalry in Ohio and one of the oldest rivalries in the nation.

All told, it was a successful festival, chairman Steve Emmel told the *Troy Daily News*. "Things went great," he said. "We had some great crowds out here and everyone had a great time. It was everything we had hoped for and more."

Chapter 13

QUEEN FOR A YEAR (AND OTHER PAGEANTS)

Throughout the history of the Troy Strawberry Festival, events have come and gone. One event that has always been part of the festival, however, is the Troy Strawberry Festival Queen's Pageant. In the forty-plus years the festival has taken place, there's always been a queen and her court to preside over the proceedings.

For decades, high school girls from around Miami County have competed to become the queen of one of the largest festivals in the Midwest. The competition has traditionally consisted of both an interview segment and talent presentation. All of the contestants also are on stage together for introductions and a group dance.

In 1977, the first year of the festival, the honor of becoming queen went to Troy High School junior Patricia Ording, daughter of Mr. and Mrs. Alton Ording. She received her tiara the night before the festival began, allowing her to attend all of the festival events—limited as they were that first year—that weekend.

Over the years, the role of the Strawberry Festival queen and her court would grow alongside the festival. When the Troy Strawberry Festival annual parade was added in 1981, the queen and her court became a focal point, riding on a strawberry-shaped float, giving pageant waves to thousands of people lining the sidewalks in downtown Troy.

For many, it created memories they'll never forget.

"In 1992, I competed to become strawberry queen," Dawn Howard said. "I walked down the aisle in a ball gown to Lionel Richie's song 'Lady.' During

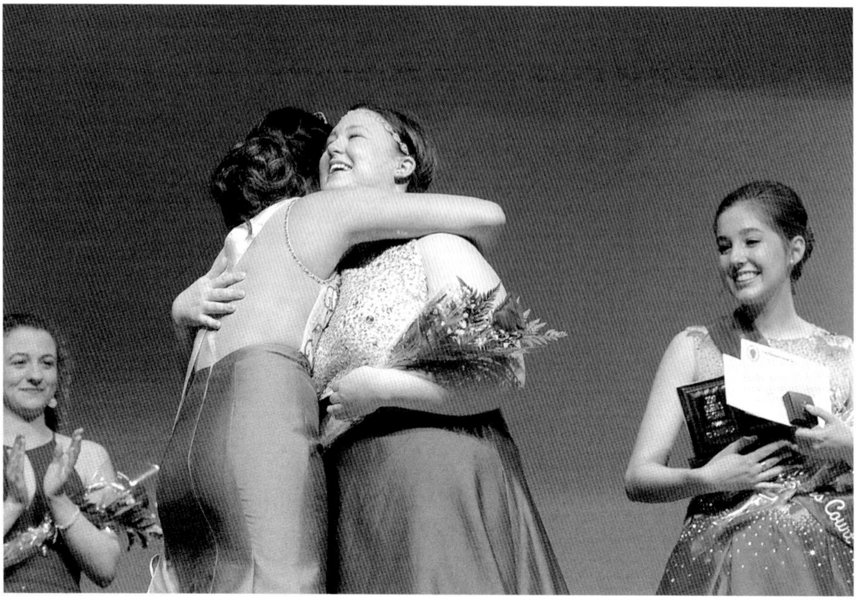

Sierra Simon is crowned 2017 Troy Strawberry Festival queen. *Courtesy of the* Troy Daily News.

competition, my speech was heard throughout the auditorium. I spoke on how my mama was my best friend and why. Though I was not elected queen, I did place and was on the queen's court.

"As strawberry royalty, we were in parades, where I waved at our small corner of the world with a wide-eyed innocence...and led many activities at the festival. It was my senior year of high school. It was a time of smiles and friendships, community and togetherness. I fondly recall the Strawberry Festival being a highlight in my young life."

As more and more events were added to the Strawberry Festival over the years, one weekend in June could no longer contain all of them. This forced festival organizers to begin staging pre-festival events, most of which took place on the weekends in May leading up to the festival.

This would expand the role of the queen and her court greatly, as part of their duties included making an appearance. Eventually, the pageant itself was moved to the spring, taking place in the Troy High School auditorium and allowing the queen and court to attend all of the pre-festival events.

The Troy Strawberry Festival Queen's Pageant has maintained its innocence over the years, as it has not been infiltrated by "professional" pageant contestants. Most of the contestants have never given any thought to entering a pageant before the Troy Strawberry Festival—and almost none compete in pageants after that.

"The year I participated in the Troy Strawberry Festival Queen's Pageant was the first, and only, time I had ever done a pageant," said 2000 Troy Strawberry Festival queen Jennie Hewitt. "I was a senior in the class of 2000 at Miami East High School and had decided not to try out for the high school musical that year, as I'd done my first three years of high school. I thought, 'Why not try something different?' It turned out to be one of the most memorable experiences of my teenage years.

"The night of the pageant was so exciting. I had no expectations of placing, let alone winning! My whole family was there to cheer me on, and I just remember being so surprised and happy that I'd made the decision to sign up. For my talent performance I sang 'Somewhere Over the Rainbow' and dressed up like Dorothy from *The Wizard of Oz*. I would be nicknamed Dorothy among the festival committee for the rest of the summer. Apparently during my song, my microphone stopped working, but I had no idea! I kept on singing like nothing was wrong (because I didn't know anything *was* wrong), and the judges later told me they were so impressed that I didn't seem fazed at all. Guess that technical malfunction worked out OK!"

Like Hewitt, most queens over the years are surprised by the crowning moment.

"It was immediate shock; I couldn't believe it, and I looked down at my mom and I could see that she was crying and so it made me really excited," said 2019 Troy Strawberry Festival queen Abby Johnson. "I've never done anything like this. I definitely was excited to step out of my comfort zone a little bit. I love singing and I love being on stage and thought I'd try something different—I definitely did not expect at all to win."

For those in attendance the night of the pageant, it's an opportunity to see a number of unique talents on display, as well. The pageant has featured traditional talents, such as singing or playing a musical instrument, but also has seen more unique talents, such as jump roping, hula hooping or delivering monologues they've written.

In 2018, queen Brook Klopfenstein's talent was playing the ukulele and singing "Stand by Me."

"I actually taught myself how to play the ukulele a couple years ago, and I loved the song and I love the message behind it. I know there's a lot going on in the world right now where we all just need to unite and come together, and I thought it was the perfect song for what's been happening this year,"

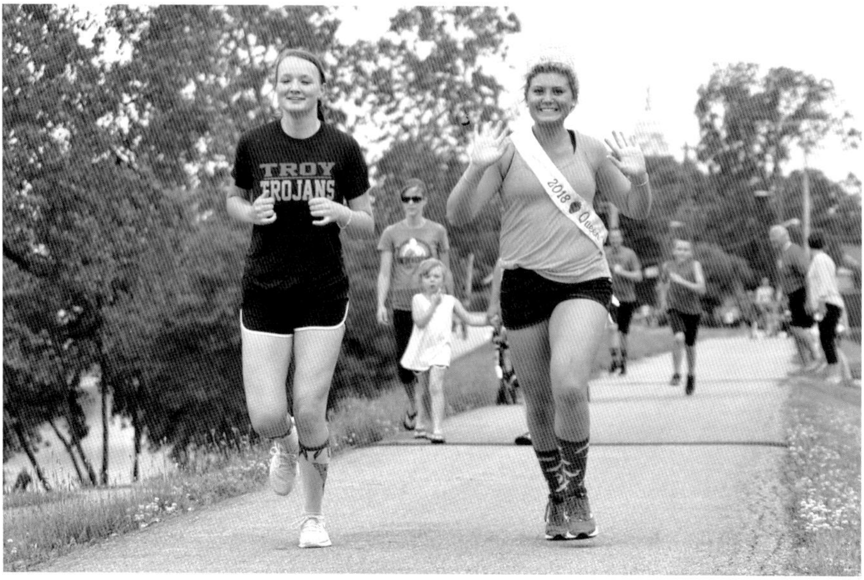

Queen's court member Cassidy Poland (*left*) and Strawberry Festival queen Brooke Klopfenstein compete in the Strawberry Festival 10K Classic. *Courtesy of the* Troy Daily News.

she said. "I look forward to walking around and seeing everything and I love talking to the little kids because they really look up to us—we're like real royalty to them. I'm just really excited to be involved in this way in my community."

When the Troy Strawberry Festival ends the first weekend in June, however, the duties of the queen and her court do not. Since the Troy Strawberry Festival is one of the first festivals of the summer, the timing allows the queen and court to make appearances at other festivals throughout the area that summer.

Truthfully, the queen is on duty through most of the entire year, up until she passes on her crown at the Strawberry Festival the following year. The queen and her court will continue to make appearances not only at other summer festivals but also at other events throughout the year, such as the city of Troy's annual Christmas tree lighting the day after Thanksgiving.

For Hewitt, being part of the pageant would extend into a large portion of her adult life. "During the summer following the pageant, I met so many great people, many of whom I'm still in contact with," she said. "I went on to chair the TSF Miss Jr. Strawberry and the Queen's Pageant for the next fifteen or so years. I never could have imagined how, even twenty years later, deciding to be in the pageant and ultimately representing Troy would become such a huge part of my life. I've always been so glad I decided to try something different."

LITTLE MISS AND MISTER STRAWBERRY

In the years following the first Troy Strawberry Festival, two more pageants were added to the festival, both of which became extremely popular over the years.

The first competition was the Little Miss and Mister Strawberry Pageant, open to students five and under. Save perhaps for the Troy Strawberry Festival Diaper Derby, few events draw as many *oohs* and *aahs* as this competition, which features youngsters in strawberry-themed outfits answering questions similar to those found on the old television show *Kids Say the Darndest Things*.

Upon receiving her crown in the 2015 competition, West Milton's Scarlette Williamson said, "I like this crown. It was fun to be on stage in my strawberry dress."

That same year, Little Mister Strawberry Devin Miller, of Casstown, said, "My favorite part was when they asked me questions and when I got this trophy."

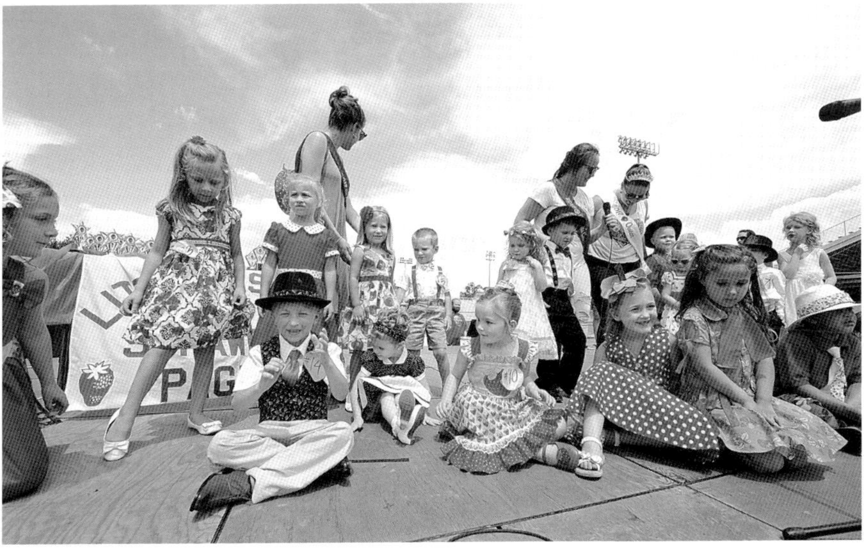

Competitors await the results at the Little Miss and Little Mister Strawberry Pageants. *Courtesy of the* Troy Daily News.

Golden Couple Competition

The Strawberry Festival Golden Couple Competition was added to the festival in the 1990s. In it, local couples who have been married fifty years or more answer *Newlywed Game*–style questions to see how well they know each other after so many years of wedded bliss.

"In 2014, Bill and I won the Golden Couple award for the Strawberry Festival," former Troy resident Carla Lohrer said. Bill Lohrer also was grand marshal of the Troy Strawberry Festival Parade in 2008. "That was a fun competition run by Mayor Michael Beamish."

In 2018, Troy's Jake and Shirley Heffner won the competition with a perfect score. "I can't believe it!" Shirley told the *Troy Daily News*, laughing at their success following the contest.

The event was often as much fun for the spectators as it was for the participants.

"My parents, Bill and Mary Ann Cusac, were named the Golden Couple for 2000," Eve Cusac Seale said. "That was the same year they celebrated fifty years of marriage on April 23! Dad was wearing his bib overalls. He insisted on wearing those even against Mother's wishes, but that was something he was very comfortable in and everyone was used to seeing him in them. He was quite the character.

"I remember sitting there on the levee watching the contest unfold. Back then, they simply asked the couples questions off the cuff, instead of the *Newlywed Game* style of questions where couples answer ahead of time and have cards with their answers. Mother was rather concerned about how Dad would respond since he was such a character. I must say, he certainly got quite a few laughs with his answers, which only encouraged him! My parents were well known around Troy and Miami County due to their work, being active with 4-H, Masons and Eastern Star. They passed away just two days apart, July 23 and 25 in 2016. My parents being honored as the Troy Strawberry Festival Golden Couple is truly my favorite highlight of all."

Chapter 14

THE FESTIVAL REACHES A TURNING POINT (2006–11)

2006

A record-setting crowd on Friday night helped kick off the thirtieth annual festival, with that momentum then carrying on throughout the weekend. Friday night was headlined by the annual Strawberry Festival Bed Races and, again, the alumni flag football game between Troy and Piqua.

"I've never seen so many people at Friday's opening night," festival chairman John Schweser said in the *Troy Daily News*. "A lot of people have told me that."

Saturday morning's parade included an entry from NASA, which featured Troy High School graduate and NASA astronaut Nancy Currie-Gregg. Saturday night's highlight was a performance by an Eagles tribute band.

"We had close to 5,000 people at the concert Saturday night, and having NASA here and Nancy Currie-Gregg, a hometown girl, riding in the parade and signing autographs made it a special weekend, I think," Schweser said.

2007

So inspiring was the Troy Strawberry Festival to one out-of-town visitor that he felt compelled to pen a song in tribute to Troy's annual showcase.

"I was at the festival last year and it was just kind of welcoming and very warm," Dan Landau, a Cincinnati resident who wrote and recorded the song "Life Is Good in Strawberryville" said in an interview with the *Troy Daily News*.

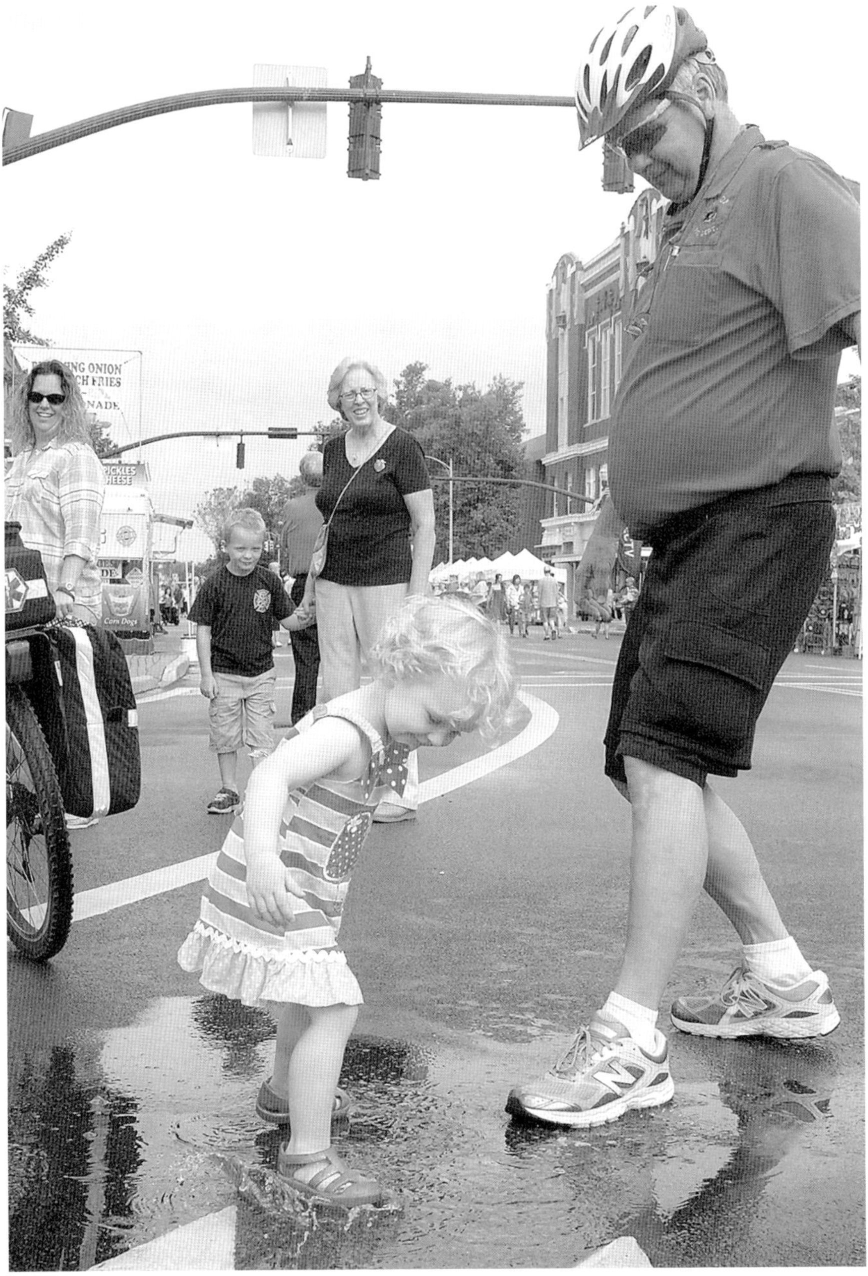

A man and child splash in a puddle during the Strawberry Festival. *Courtesy of the* Troy Daily News.

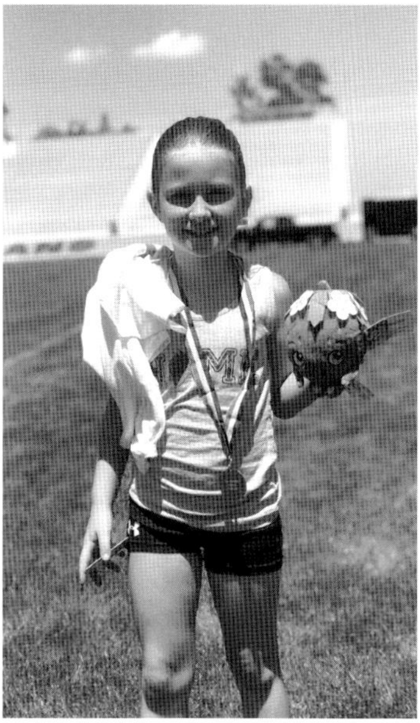

A young lady proudly shows off her Strawberry Festival medal. *Courtesy of the Garrity family.*

"It really seemed like a good place to go and forget about the troubles of the world. It really represented a place where everything seemed to be just fine in the midst of all the bad stuff in the news. So I wrote about that."

The song was a perfect fit for the festival's Jimmy Buffett–inspired theme of "Strawberryville."

"He called and said he'd written the song, and the first thing I thought of was, 'He's trying to sell me a song or sell his song up on the levee,'" festival chairman Tom Cooney said in an interview with the *Troy Daily News*. "But the more I talked to him, I saw that wasn't what he had in mind at all. He said he had written a song so good that he wanted it to be used and wanted to know if I would be interested. He dropped it off and I played it…and it's really good."

In the early evening on Saturday, weather once again played a factor in the festival, as lightning touched down on festival grounds, injuring several festival attendees. The strike came just after country singer Mandy Neff had finished performing at the festival's main stage.

"A light rain started, then we got a lightning strike near the center of the festival," Troy Police Department captain Joe Long said in the *Troy Daily News*. "Things were really coming at us at that point. We were trying to get more medics down there to get the injured people to the hospital."

Fortunately, nobody was seriously injured, although the storms did bring a premature end to the festival.

2008

Weather again played a factor in the Troy Strawberry Festival, as rain forced the Troy Police Department to shut down the levee for a portion of the day Saturday. Then, temperatures soaring into the nineties on Sunday kept some would-be festivalgoers away.

Still, though, festival chairman Fred Daffner deemed the weekend a success.

"All in all, it turned out pretty successful," Daffner said.

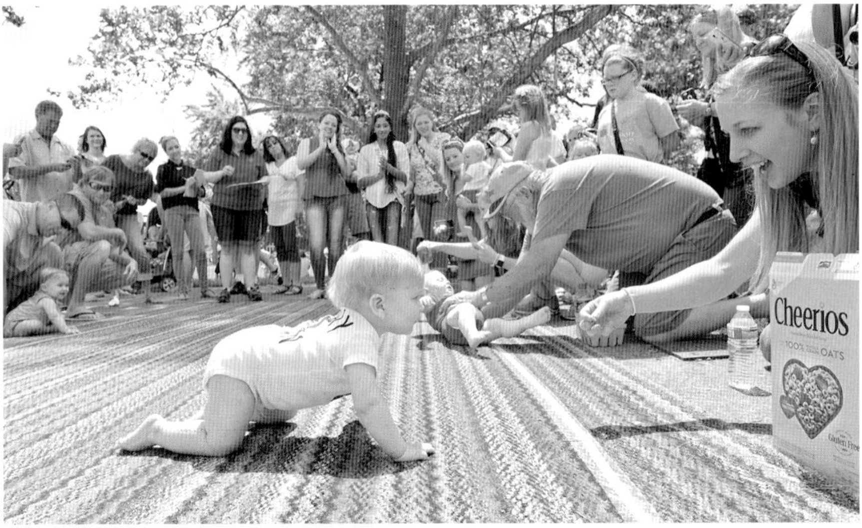

A Diaper Derby contestant races for a Cheerio. *Courtesy of the* Troy Daily News.

2009

Finally, after several years in a row of inclement weather, the Troy Strawberry Festival again drew a break in 2009 with perfect weather all weekend.

"Everything has went fabulous," festival chairwoman Becky Pappas said in an interview with the *Troy Daily News*. "Clubs, vendors and organizations are saying they had a great turnout. I think it was one of the biggest crowds we've had in years. I think some of the booths sold out and I think it was because the weather was just fabulous."

2010

One year after Becky Pappas served as festival chairwoman, her husband, Dave, got his hand at chairing the Troy Strawberry Festival.

The weather wasn't quite as hospitable for Dave. Rains shut down the festival at one point, forced the annual rubber duck race from the Great Miami River to the Troy Aquatic Park and canceled a kayak event.

Of course, the weather probably didn't bother the couple, as they have spent years running the Troy Strawberry Festival Soccer Invitational, which itself has seen numerous weather-related adjustments over the years.

"You should be proud," Dave Pappas told the crowd that had gathered for the Friday Night Kickoff events, highlighted by the bed races and big wheel races. "Troy is really fortunate. There are a lot of great events planned this weekend on the levee."

2011

The sun shone again at the Strawberry Festival, allowing for big crowds and bigger profits for local nonprofit organizations in 2011.

"That was my biggest concern, the weather," 2011 festival chairman Dave Geiger said in an interview with the *Troy Daily News*. "The weather was good, attendance was good. You never know how much goes into the festival. It really opened my eyes. But it was a good time. A fun experience."

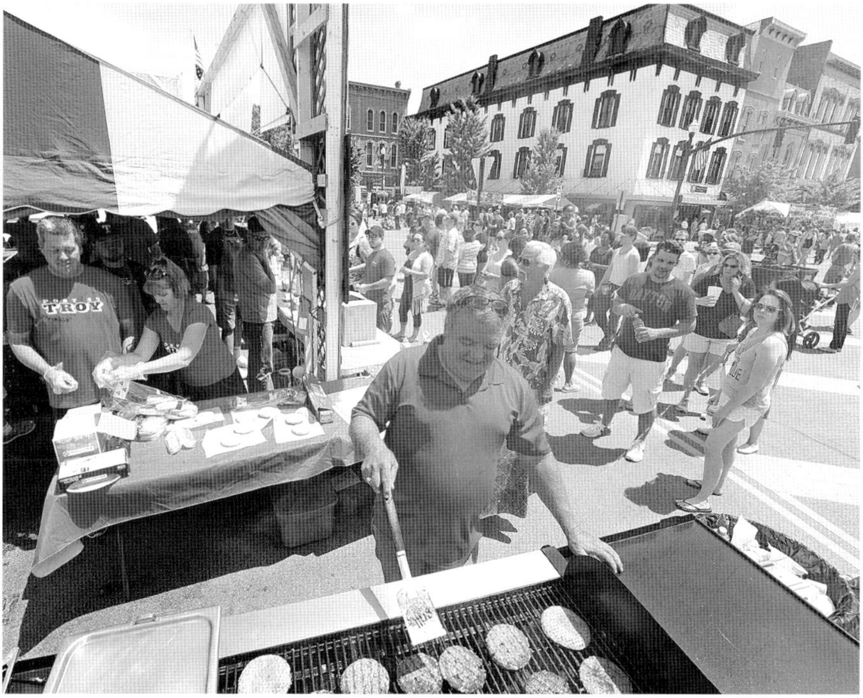

Food is grilled on the square during the Troy Strawberry Festival. *Courtesy of the* Troy Daily News.

Chapter 15

A FESTIVAL UNLIKE ANY OTHER (2012)

In 2012, the Troy Strawberry Festival faced a challenge unlike any it had ever seen before in its history. But where others may have seen obstacles, then–Strawberry Festival manager Heather Dorsten saw opportunities.

"This is going to be a fun year," Dorsten said in an interview with the *Troy Daily News* prior to the start of the 2012 Troy Strawberry Festival. "It's really a unique opportunity. I know myself and [2012 Troy Strawberry Festival chairwoman] Corie Schweser are excited."

The year prior, immediately following the 2011 Troy Strawberry Festival, the Adams Street Bridge in Troy was closed for repairs. Since the first one in 1977, the Troy Strawberry Festival had been held on the Great Miami Valley River levee area between the Market Street Bridge and Adams Street Bridge. With the closing of the Adams Street Bridge, holding the festival at its traditional home no longer was an option.

A number of other options were explored, including moving the festival to the Miami County Fairgrounds or even shutting down the festival for one year, but eventually Dorsten and the rest of the festival organizers decided to hold the festival in downtown Troy for one year only.

That was the original plan, at least. In 2013, the festival would move back to the levee, but ultimately in 2014 it was decided to split the festival between the levee and downtown locations, with the majority of the booths being placed in downtown Troy.

The decision in 2012 to move the festival downtown would essentially create a seismic shift in festival philosophy. The accessibility downtown to

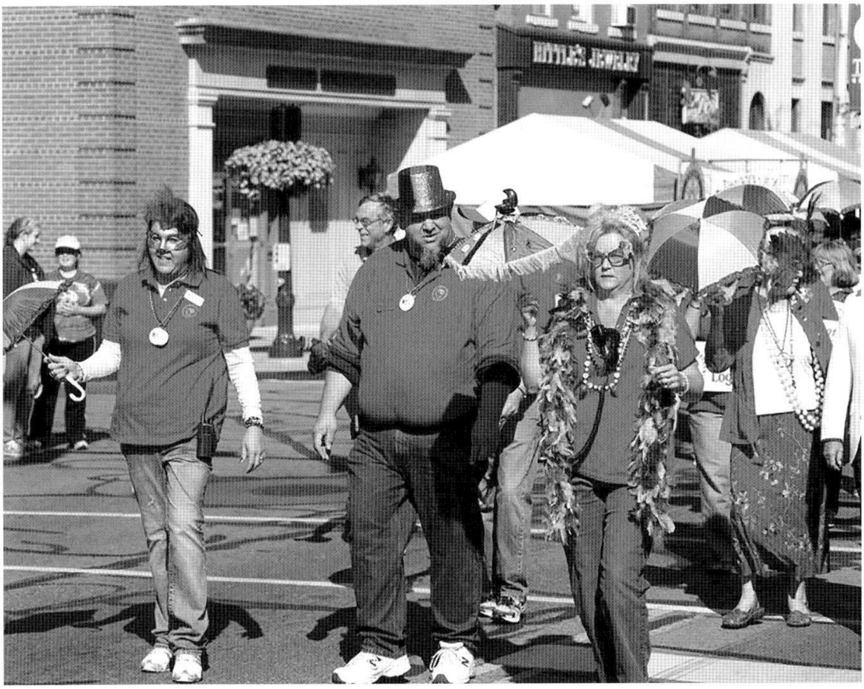

The 2012 Troy Strawberry Festival featured a Mardi Gras theme. *Courtesy of Roberta Jacobs.*

cars and shuttle buses, coupled with the opportunity for downtown shops to benefit, and paved streets, making it easier to push strollers and wheelchairs, showed festival organizers the benefits of the move. To this day, the festival continues to be a yearly downtown staple.

"I knew when I took over as the festival manager in 2011 the bridge would be out, but I was told we would do our best to keep it on the levee," Dorsten said. "Once we figured out that wouldn't be an option, we had to start looking at other opportunities."

One idea that continually came up in the public was moving the festival outside city limits—the Miami County Fairgrounds are located just outside Troy city limits—but it was an idea Dorsten and her staff were not willing to entertain. "We wanted to keep it within the city limits," Dorsten said prior to the 2012 festival. "The festival will still be in Troy, just right across the river. We can easily move it back to the levee next year. Logistically, we've had a lot of people from the city who have donated their time to the festival for many years. Our facilities guys are all from the city and know the festival like the back of their hand. We wanted them to be able to continue to help us out with the festival—some of them have been with us from the very beginning."

Moving the festival downtown meant organizers had to deal with a number of challenges in preparing for the festival.

"The biggest thing was the logistics and learning about what you can and can't do on the city streets," Dorsten said. "There are many more rules and regulations that you have to follow. It was interesting, to say the least. The levee was upgraded for electrical and water usage in the early 2000s. With the festival moving downtown, we had to worry about getting electrical generators and making use of hydrants. All of our biggest electric users had to be moved to the side streets, closer to the generators.

"There is so much more security that you need having the festival downtown. We needed at least fifteen more volunteers than we'd needed in previous years."

Parking, too, was a challenge unlike any previous festival had faced, Dorsten said. That year, the festival had to increase the use of shuttle buses—provided by the Troy City Schools—to bus in festivalgoers from WACO Airfield, the fairgrounds and several parking lots around town.

"We actually held a car show over at the fairgrounds to give people something to do and further encourage them to use the shuttle buses," Dorsten said. "We were strongly encouraging people to take the shuttle to the festival that year. It's something we had always done in the past, as parking has been difficult at the festival for years, but it is something we definitely had to encourage more than ever when we moved the festival downtown."

Dorsten said she knew going in the festival wouldn't look like it had in previous years, but every effort was made to include as many traditional events as possible. A number of events traditionally held during the festival weekend—including the Golden Couple and Little Mister and Miss Strawberry Competitions—were held prior to the festival.

Some competitions were canceled for that year. In some cases, those cancelations became permanent, as festival organizers were able to assess and overhaul the event roster.

"A lot of Troy Memorial Stadium events, like the Backseat Driver Competition, we weren't able to have," Dorsten said. "But we still had all the little kid events, like the diaper derby and big wheel races. We still had the pie-eating competition. We still had the bed races, but we moved them from the downtown area [on Friday night] to the Hobart Arena parking lot."

The bed races, which had traditionally been the most popular event on the Friday Night Kickoff to the festival, did move to the Hobart Arena

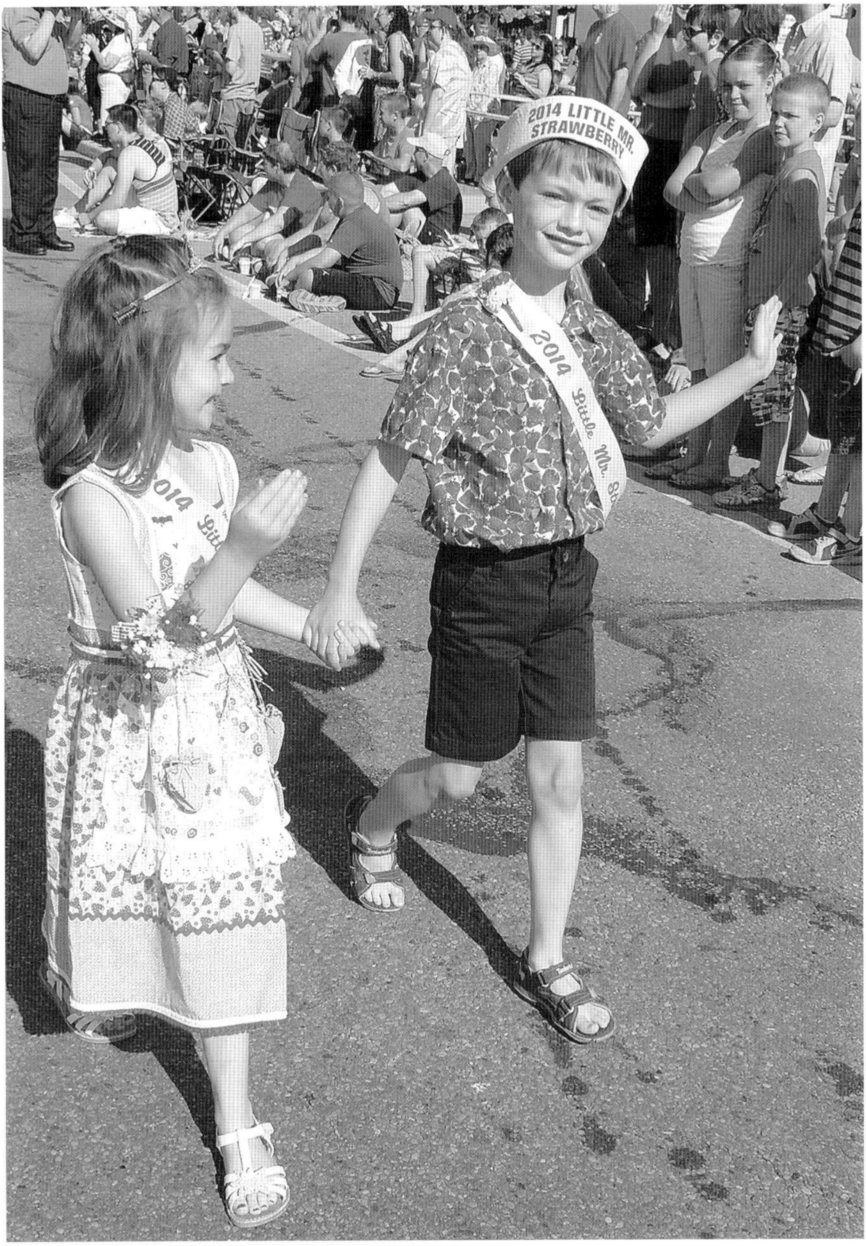

Jayla Leeland (*left*), 2014 Little Miss Strawberry, and 2014 Little Mister Strawberry Matthew Waller greet their fans. *Courtesy of the* Troy Daily News.

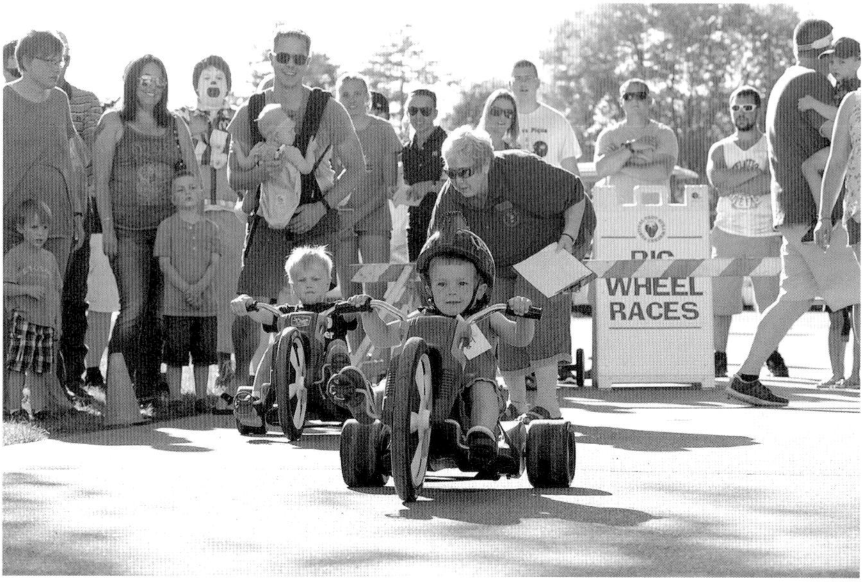

Racers compete in the big wheel races. *Courtesy of the* Troy Daily News.

parking lot but never truly recovered the popularity they once had. The sight of teams pushing beds on wheels around the fountain in the Troy town square as thousands lined the streets and sidewalks to watch never could be re-created in an empty parking lot.

Dorsten said the majority of food and craft vendors, staples of the annual event, were generally supportive of the move downtown. That would hold true as subsequent festivals were split between downtown and the levee.

"Most of them didn't back out," Dorsten said in a 2012 interview with the *Troy Daily News*. "There will still be most of the food and crafts people are used to. There hasn't been a lot of panic."

While the move downtown definitely presented some challenges, Dorsten said, it also provided some opportunities that ultimately made downtown Troy a festival fixture. "First and foremost, it gave people the opportunity to see our beautiful downtown," she said. "Also, if it rains, there are a lot more places to duck into…and we don't have to worry about mud on our city streets. It also gives people a chance to duck inside a building and get out of the heat when it's a warm weekend. For example, we moved our emergency services into the Hayner Cultural Center, which has air conditioning. I know our emergency services people were happy about that."

Chapter 16

CLUBS AND ORGANIZATIONS

Perhaps lost in all of the pageantry, sometimes forgotten in the revelry and hidden by the annual hoopla is the real reason the Troy Strawberry Festival was born more than four decades ago. For all the fun it brings to the community, the primary reason the Strawberry Festival was created was as a way for nonprofit organizations in Troy to raise money. For many organizations, the festival is a vital source of income. For some, it's the only fundraiser they need to sustain themselves throughout the year.

"That's the whole reason the festival was started…it was for the nonprofits," said Doug Trostle, who was part of the committee that put together the first Troy Strawberry Festival in 1977 and was the second festival chairman in 1978. "A lot of the clubs and organizations needed a way to raise money. This was a way to bring people together and have them all in one place so those clubs and organizations would have the opportunity to raise money. I think there are a lot of people who may have lost sight of that over the years, but that was the original intent of the festival."

One of the most popular nonprofit booths over the years has been The Future Begins Today's strawberry salsa booth. Originally developed and introduced by former The Future Begins Today executive director Cheryl Cotner, the salsa—which many describe as having a "sweet heat" flavor—sells out every year, with the money raised going to the foundation's scholarship programs.

"The yummy and crowd-pleasing Strawberry Sweet Heat Salsa was inspired by the community's love and tradition surrounding the Troy

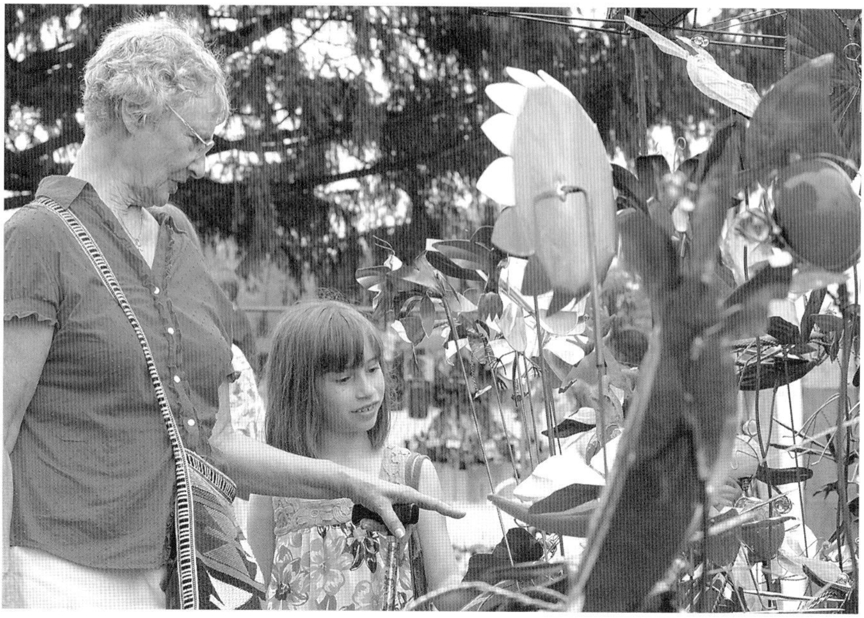

Festival attendees get a closer look at the crafts selection. *Courtesy of the* Troy Daily News.

Strawberry Festival," former Troy Future Begins Today executive director Natalie Rohlfs said. Rohlfs also was a member of the Strawberry Festival Queen's Court in the late 1990s. "More than a decade and a half ago, Strawberry Salsa was first sold by the nonprofit organization The Future Begins Today and has continued to be a festival favorite since, with each purchase supporting scholarship opportunities for Troy students. It's even received two Strawberry Festival Culinary Awards. We love the Strawberry Festival, the people it draws to our town, the students it helps support and the eighty volunteers who work with our booth each year."

Another one of the most popular food attractions at the festival is the Troy Senior Citizens Center's strawberry shortcakes. The shortcakes are not only popular because they are so tasty but also because they have been traditionally sold inside the Troy Senior Citizens Center—which sits on the east end of the Great Miami River levee—and it is air conditioned, providing one of the few places festival attendees could find relief from the heat and humidity over the years.

While it may be great for those consuming the strawberry shortcakes, it's hard work for those preparing them. "I have worked at the Senior Citizens Center strawberry shortcake sale for several years," Claudia Freed

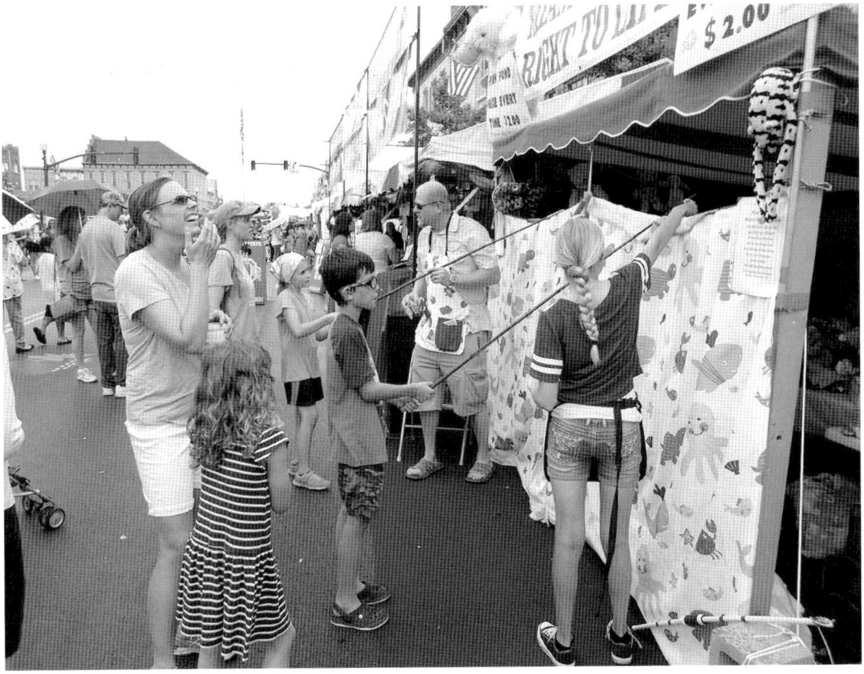

The Miami County Right to Life Organization runs its "fishpond" in downtown Troy. *Courtesy of the Enneking family.*

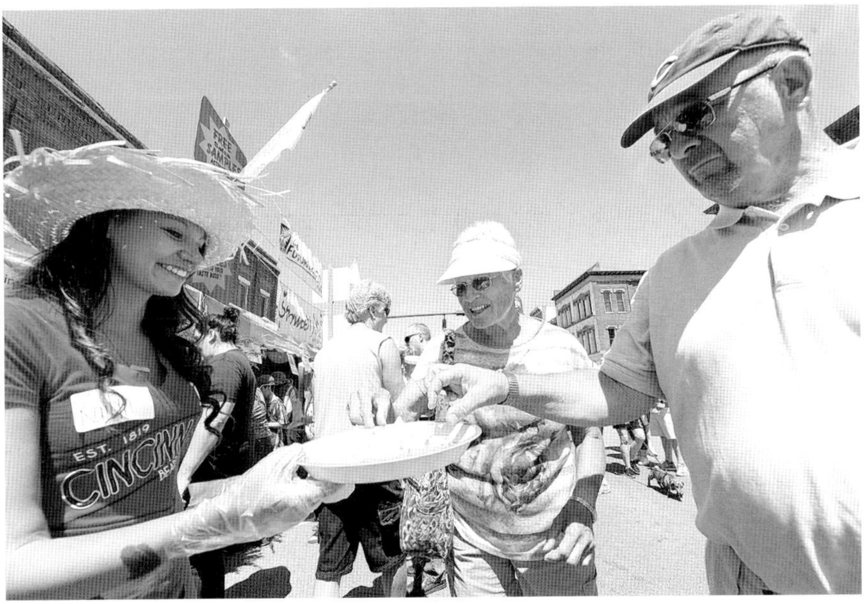

A couple samples the The Future Begins Today's strawberry salsa. *Courtesy of the* Troy Daily News.

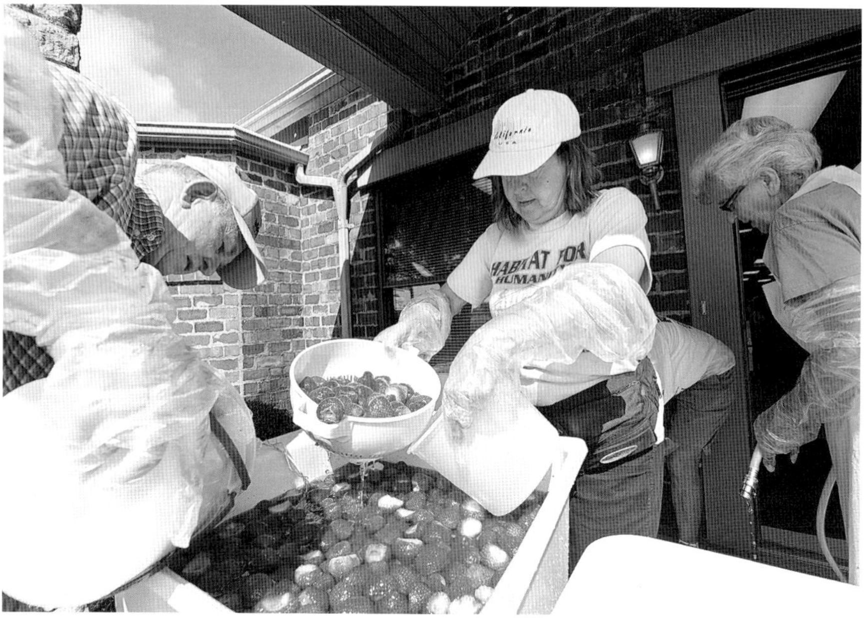

Members of the Troy Senior Citizens Center prepare berries for their famous strawberry shortcakes. *Courtesy of the* Troy Daily News.

Schertzinger said. "It takes lots of preparation. First, 1,200 pounds of strawberries have to be cleaned. Then they are washed several times before going to the slicer. From there, the berries are mixed. They are refrigerated until needed. It takes quite a few people to get this all done.

"The strawberry shortcakes are a big moneymaker for the center every year, and there is always a line waiting to get in the center. The best part of working the sale is the people and their stories. I have had people from out of state and others who came as children with their parents and now bring their children. I have had people tell me they come to the festival just for the shortcake. The craft ladies also sell their crafts at the festival, which is also a great moneymaker for the center."

Over the years, most of the Troy High School athletic programs, as well as local youth sports teams, have benefited from the opportunity to open booths at the festival and make money. For some of those sports, the chance to have a booth at the festival is key in funding the program.

"I am not exactly sure of the year the team started selling hot dogs and brats, but I think it was the third or fourth year," said former Troy wrestler and current Troy High School wrestling assistant coach Chris Behm. "The booth is operated by the Troy Wrestling Parents Club. When it [the festival] was on the levee, I worked it in the late '90s as a wrestler. Parents always grilled, and we were the cashiers. The money raised over the years [has] paid for mats, uniforms and camps. Because we have been at it for so long, we got a great spot on the square when the festival moved, right in front of what is now Haren's Meat Market. The last several years, Connor Haren, a wrestling alum, has supplied brats and hot dogs to the team. He also made a strawberry brat we sell that has become the bestseller."

Since every booth at the Strawberry Festival is different—and since so many people in Troy are members of more than one team or organization—many people have worked at a number of different booths over the years and have learned how to sell a wide variety of items to hungry consumers. Typically, the more booths at which a Troy resident worked means more memories created over the years.

"I wrestled varsity in grades seven through twelve and played varsity football in eleventh and twelfth grades, which means I spent a lot of time involved in the Strawberry Festival," Craig Kitchen said. "My dad, Nick Kitchen, was the wrestling parent organization president for two years, so

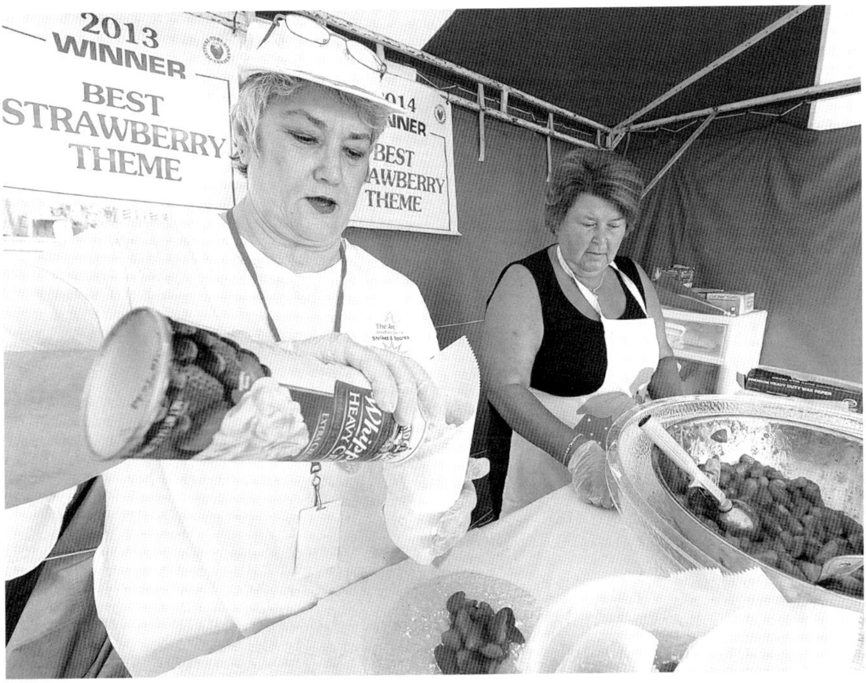

Workers prepare strawberry chimichangas. *Courtesy of the* Troy Daily News.

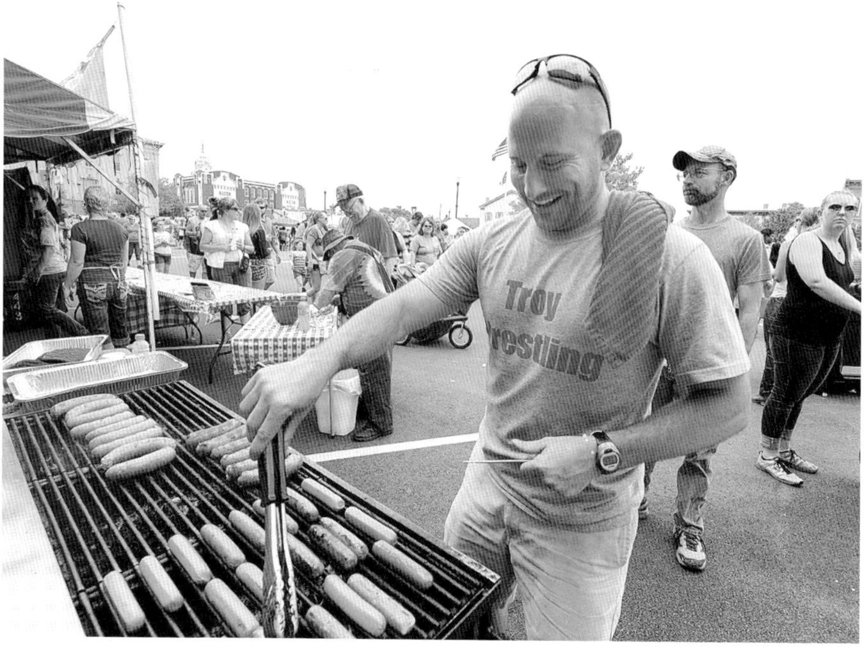

Troy wrestling coach Doug Curnes works the grill for the Troy Wrestling Parents Association. *Courtesy of the* Troy Daily News.

I had double duty. I remember my dad and I taking an old camper and gutting and painting it to make a cheap, enclosed trailer to store and haul all the grills, refrigerators, tables and the tent we used at the festival to raise money for the team.

"I remember going to Fulton Farms and picking berries for both football and wrestling, eating more than we picked, and on occasions have a strawberry fight with Bubba Smith and LeVen Stafford. Good times. I remember spending the nights at the festival to keep our booth safe, helping ourselves to the hot dogs, brats and a couple chocolate-covered strawberries. The football guys and wrestling guys would get together and hang out on the levee, and as a junior, hanging out with the seniors like Bobby Rohlfs, Eddie Guillozet and Doug Fessler. These guys were a great influence on me, and I can also call them my friends. I remember getting up early on those Saturday mornings to get those wonderful strawberry donuts hot out of the grease, and then back and forth to each booth, football and wrestling, helping out. Then there was the canoe races and softball tournament—so much work but at the same time so much fun. Looking back on those days at the festival really taught me a lot, and I thank Troy for those opportunities."

For many young Troy residents, their first experience entering the "workforce" was volunteering at the Troy Strawberry Festival.

"All three of my daughters' first jobs were volunteer working the church booth for strawberry shortcakes," Bandie Cruea said. "This taught them work ethics before becoming teenagers and holding real, paying jobs. After their shifts, we would then walk the festival and shop or eat or whatever. Great memories!"

Working the strawberry festival often was a family affair, with parents working right alongside their children to help raise money. Alicia McMullen-Smith remembers helping her dad, Fred McMullen, legendary Troy baseball coach, raise money for his teams.

"My dad ran the speed booth for years," she said. "I remember working it with him and always trying to win my age bracket. Fastest pitch for each age bracket. The money went to support the baseball team."

One of the reasons strawberries were selected to represent the festival when it started in 1977 was their versatility. Over the years, the red fruit has been used in just about every way imaginable, including many no one likely would have thought of had it not been for the festival. One of the most popular booths over the years has been the strawberry burrito booth.

"I think my family and I have been in almost every part of the festival," Sandy Jean Smith Hall said. "We have been in the parade, did floats, both my children were in the berry crawl, the Little Mister and Miss Pageants, my daughter did the donuts, then we worked on the canoes for the Arc of Miami County. When the levee washed out, we needed a new booth, so one year we did a kids' booth. Then we were given the task of making the strawberry burritos and still do this every year. This was our biggest fundraiser, and it brought awareness to our organization. We also won our share of awards and have been on TV and in magazines for our burritos. I have been to every festival since it started."

Granted, all of those strawberry dishes require lots of, well, strawberries.

"I also remember picking tons of strawberries, then cleaning them and making strawberry crepes with my mom for her sorority to sell at the festival,'" Yonnie Travis said.

Of course, not everything sold at the Troy Strawberry Festival is based around the plump red fruit. There are other food offerings for those who don't necessarily want something with a strawberry flavor to it.

"Our Boy Scout Troop 544 sold corn on the cob for years," Susie Roeth Norman said. "The dads would cook it down below the booth near the stadium, and moms and boys would butter it and sell it for one dollar an ear."

Unfortunately, not every booth turned into a moneymaker for the local nonprofits, and some had to be altered or even abandoned over the years. Even when booths stop vending at the festival, however, most who participated are glad they were able to do so.

"My nonprofit sorority worked the festival from day one, and the last year was 2011," Mary DeHart said. "We started out with a fishing booth for children. We then changed to food—hamburgers, hot dogs, sloppy joes and nachos. Over the last few years, we were not making the money needed due to more and more food vendors. Also a few years of bad weather. Just breaking even wasn't worth all the work since most of us were senior citizens. We made money to give back to the community, and that just wasn't happening. We did have some great years, and we were thankful for that."

In addition to the nonprofit booths, most of which sell food, the festival also has featured independent craft vendors selling their wares since the festival began. The festival has featured thousands of different craft booths, which have been some of its most popular draws. As always, the Troy Strawberry Festival tries to have a little something for everyone.

"My dear mother, Jeanne Massie, had a lovely booth that my dad, Roger Massie, built for her arts and crafts that she would sell at craft shows," Susan Christian Liddy said. "She did beautiful copper enameled jewelry, and she made designs and put them on wood for a decoration. She was very talented and did beautiful work. She sold her designs at the Troy Strawberry Festival starting in 1977. I remember she did quite well in her sales because her designs were so unique and there was nothing else like it there at the time. She always enjoyed the festival so much, as she was born and raised in Troy. Her father, Eugene Smick, was the Troy police chief for many years, retiring in the late 1950s. She really knew her Troy history and had many friends in Troy."

For some festivalgoers, the booths at the Troy Strawberry Festival afforded them opportunities to win big. "One Friday night while on the square waiting for the bed races, we walked around to get something to eat," John Mathes said. "We passed a booth selling rubber ducks for the duck race. I bought a duck and forgot about it. Sunday night we were watching TV, and I got a call and the lady said, 'Mr. Mathes, you won a truck in the duck race and I am leaving town in the morning, so call Dave Arbogast to pick it up.' I first thought it was a friend or family member pranking me, but I called and it was true; I had won the truck in the duck race."

While the booths at the Strawberry Festival have raised money for some and given trucks to others, what they have provided more than anything

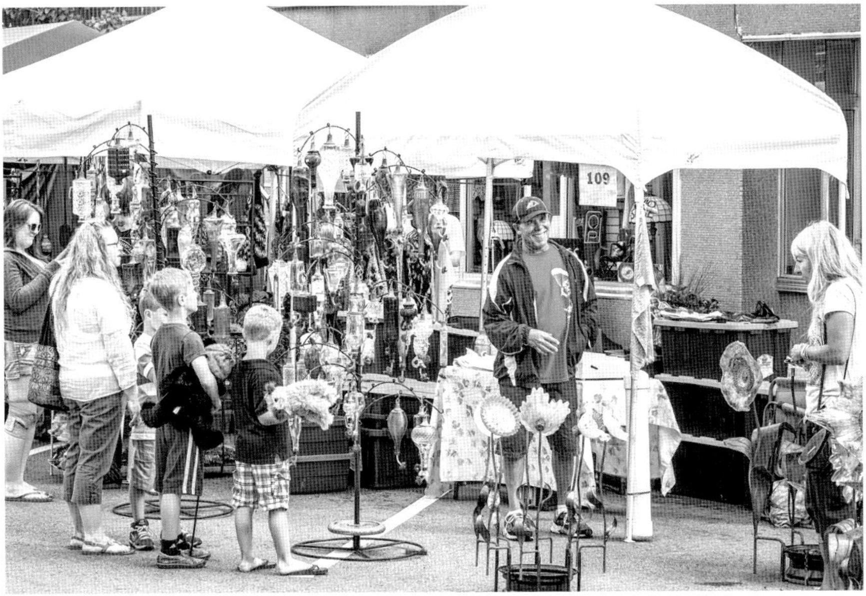

Craft vendors show their wares. *Courtesy of the* Troy Daily News.

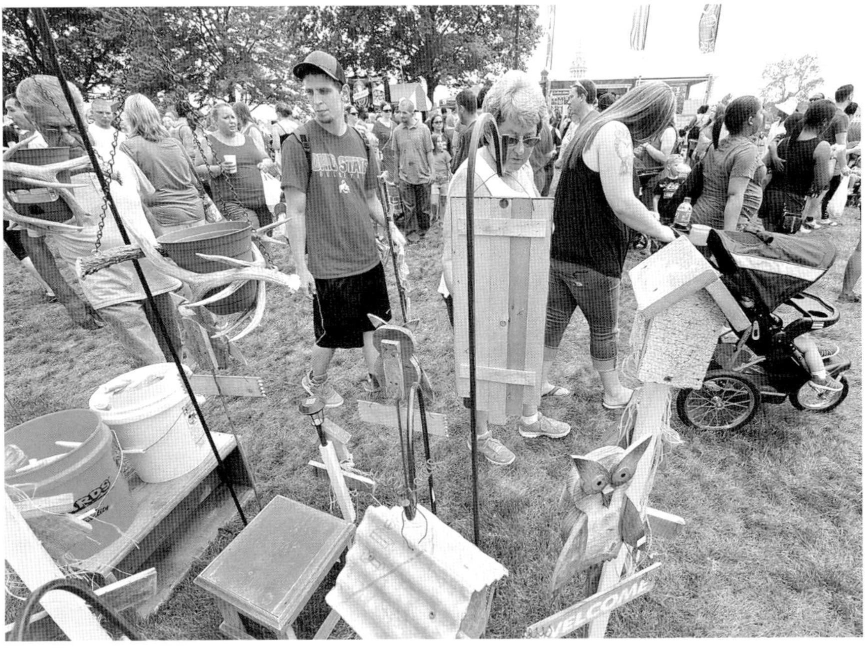

There are always plenty of crafts to see at the Strawberry Festival. *Courtesy of the* Troy Daily News.

over the years is memories for those who have worked at them. In some cases, those are cherished memories, even when things don't work out quite as planned.

"I was a freshman at Troy High School at the time my friend Bonita and I were running the cotton candy machine," Tammy P. Britton said. "We had no idea how to run the machine. People kept returning for a refund because the middle of the cotton candy cone was as hard as a rock. Bonita and I had no idea how to fix it. I think her and I lost more money for that booth than we made that year. Fun times in the 1970s!"

Chapter 17

THE FESTIVAL TODAY (2013–PRESENT)

2013

The festival did return to the levee in 2013, and the parade returned as well. It would end up being both the final year the festival was held exclusively on the levee and the final year of the parade.

Poor weather didn't help the early part of the festival in 2013, but as has always been the case, the festival would continue with an air of optimism. The weather would improve by Sunday, as did the crowds.

"We had a great day," festival chairman Jon Dankworth said in an interview with the *Troy Daily News*. "I think it went a lot better than we thought it would. Friday with the rain, I thought, 'Oh no, what if it's this way all weekend?' But it seemed like there was some sort of bubble over Troy, and every time the radar showed rain, it was dissipating."

One of the highlights of the festival that year was a series of performances by the Troy Pop Rocks Jump Rope Team. The team, which has performed at halftime of high school and college basketball games across the country, including The Ohio State University, Duke University, the University of Tennessee and the University of Wisconsin, put on a special performance for the delegation from Takahashi City.

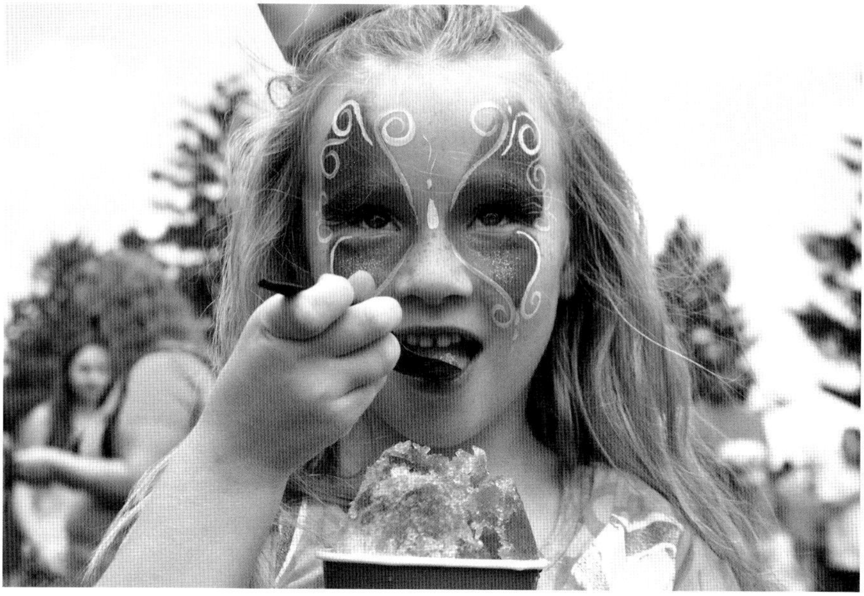

A girl wearing butterfly face paint enjoys a snow cone. *Courtesy of the* Troy Daily News.

2014

In 2014, the Strawberry Festival split the difference between the two locations—downtown Troy and the levee—with the majority of the booths and events taking place downtown. The festival has continued to operate at both locations ever since. Holding it in two locations gave the festival twice the space for festival attendees to spread out.

"I think things went really well," festival chairwoman Kathi Roetter said in an interview with the *Troy Daily News*. "We don't have any crowd estimates yet, but we do feel like Saturday was a record number. There were just people everywhere, so we definitely think it was a record crowd."

Roetter would eventually go on to become the full-time festival manager following her stint in 2014.

2015

Sunny skies and mild temperatures were the perfect recipe for a sellout weekend in 2015. Several clubs and organizations ran out of products on Sunday afternoon—or as early as Saturday evening. The Future Begins

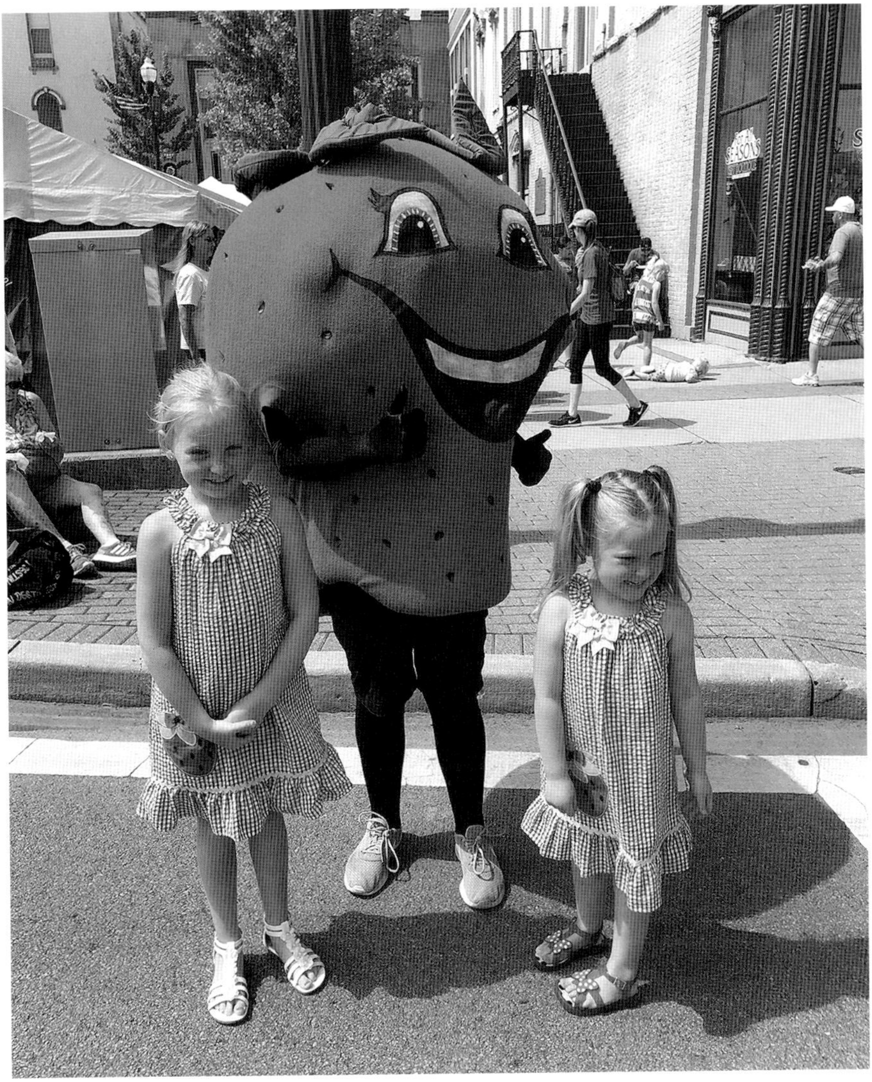

The Bigelow sisters, Baylee and Ellee, visit with a giant strawberry. *Courtesy of the Bigelow family.*

Today booth sold out of its famous strawberry salsa at the festival and had to close shop. Newton Band Boosters sold 17,028 quarts of fresh strawberries on Saturday alone. The organization was completely shut down on Sunday due to running out of its fresh strawberry supply.

"It's going really well—everyone is selling out of food which is a great problem to have," festival chairwoman Corie Schweser said in an interview with the *Troy Daily News*. "We had two beautiful days in a row with more and more people are selling out by the hour."

More than seventeen thousand dozen strawberry doughnuts were sold from the Troy Music Band Boosters on Saturday.

2016

The 2016 anniversary of the Troy Strawberry Festival saw much of what past festivals had seen throughout the previous four decades: a healthy amount of rain. Still, though, that was not enough to keep the crowds away as the festival pushed on, just as it always has through the years.

"After a little bit of rain Saturday, today turned out beautiful," festival chairman Nathan Walters said in an interview with the *Troy Daily News*. "It turned out to be a pretty good weekend overall. I am thankful for the sponsors and volunteers, the festivalgoers, the arts and crafts vendors and the non-profits," he said. "They have all been fantastic to work with."

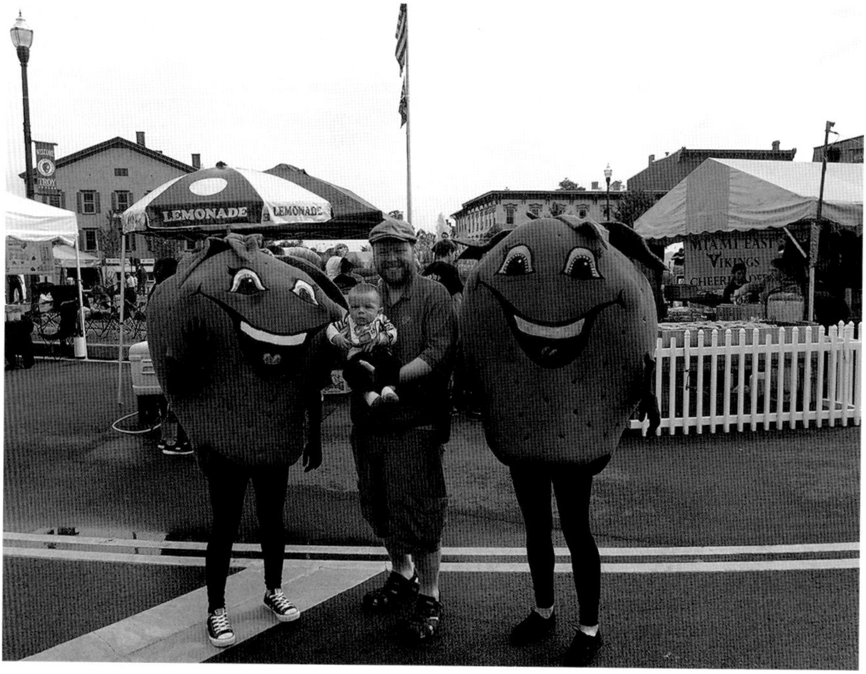

Former Troy Strawberry Festival chairman Nathan Walters holds his son Toby. *Courtesy of Melissa Walters.*

2017

The theme for the 2017 Troy Strawberry Festival was "Silver Screen Berries," and the entire weekend had a movie theme surrounding it.

And perfect skies above it.

"After two years of planning…to see everything come together without a hitch," festival chairman Matt Watkins said in an interview with the *Troy Daily News*. "I'm very particular, so seeing everything go off as it did will help me sleep very well tonight. We purposely put a lot of recognizable movie-themed items out and kept movie-themed songs going to keep the theme going even if it was just the background music," he said. "We wanted people to feel like they were at a movie premiere."

Amidst all the hoopla, the festival also featured a marriage proposal when Troy resident DeWayne Williams proposed to Amanda Gibson. "You have been on my case for two weeks now, saying, 'You've got something going on. You're sneaky, none of my friends will talk to me,'" Williams said to the crowd who was waiting for the entertainment for the evening to begin. "You can put that to ease now. I love you with all my heart. You are my universe, you are my stars, you are my sunshine. There's no one else I'd rather do it with, you and our three beautiful children," Williams said. "So what I'm trying to say is, will you marry me?"

Gibson said yes, adding just a little more lore to the historic festival.

2018

The traditional Friday night events moved from downtown Troy to Troy's Treasure Island, taking advantage of the recent construction of an amphitheater near the banks of the Great Miami River.

"Friday night, I felt was everything I was looking for," Festival chairman Eric Roetter said in an interview with the *Troy Daily News*.

That momentum would continue through the weekend, as more perfect weather prevailed, leading to huge crowds and a profitable two days for the local nonprofits.

"The MVP for Strawberry Festival weekend was Mother Nature," Roetter said. "I couldn't have asked for a more perfect weekend. From Friday to Sunday, to be exact. My year was only going to be as successful as the weather cooperating—and my year was successful because of that."

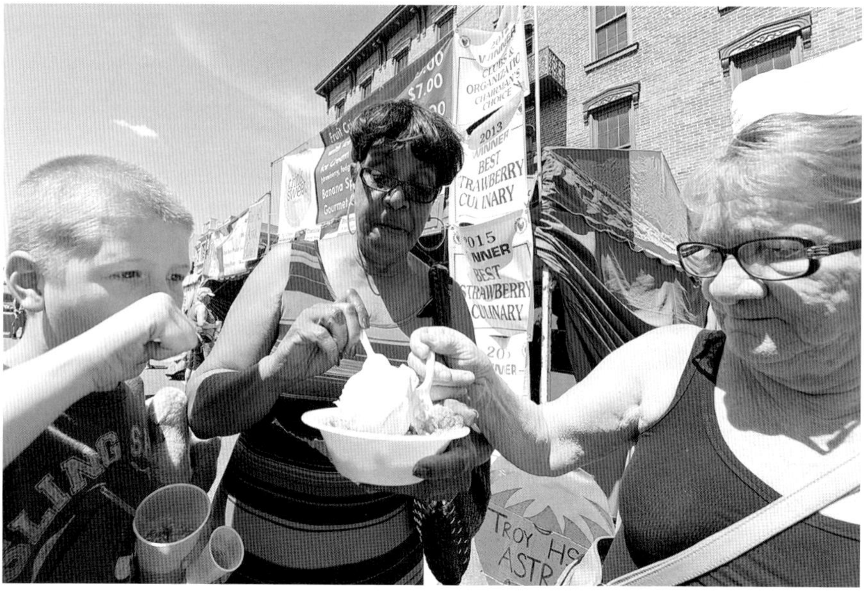

A family shares strawberry ice cream. *Courtesy of the* Troy Daily News.

2019

The 2019 Troy Strawberry Festival started slow, likely because of a rainy forecast, but finished with a flourish Sunday.

"Sunday made up for everything," festival chairman Bruce Adamson said in an interview with the *Troy Daily News*. "Lots of vendors sold out on Sunday. One arts and crafts vendor said this is the first year he actually had fun," said Adamson, who said some new procedures put in place this year helped. "No negative comments, that's always good."

At the time, no one could possibly have known it would be the last Troy Strawberry Festival anyone would see for more than a year.

2020

Like so many other things in 2020, the Troy Strawberry Festival was canceled as a result of health and safety concerns created by the COVID-19 global pandemic.

"We knew we had to make a decision earlier than later," Troy Chamber of Commerce executive director and Troy Strawberry Festival manager

Kathi Roetter said in an April interview with the *Troy Daily News*. "We had talked about the idea [of] postponing, but from a logistics point, it wasn't possible. We are continuing to talk about what we can do throughout the year and gathering ideas and getting creative to support the nonprofits. We hope our nonprofits can partner with other festivals and other events later in the summer and into the fall. We'll have to do things a little differently and come back bigger and better in 2021.

"We extend our sincere appreciation to the members of the festival committee as they prepared for the festival over the past year, as well as our non-profit organizations, arts and craft vendors, performers and sponsors who were primed to celebrate with us," said Linda Roth, chairwoman of the 2020 Troy Strawberry Festival, in an interview with the *Troy Daily News*. "Our priority continues to be the health and safety of our volunteers, guests and all festival supporters, and as such, we are following the recommendations of national and global health experts."

Chapter 18

BEHIND THE SCENES AT THE STRAWBERRY FESTIVAL

Once a year, on the evening of the first Sunday in June, Kathi Roetter allows herself to stop and take a deep breath, enjoy the moment and relax.

Then she gets back to work.

The Troy Strawberry Festival may take place the first full weekend in June, but most of the planning for it takes the better part of the prior year. There are some parts of the planning, such as selecting the general chairperson, that take place several years in advance.

Planning a festival that can see anywhere between 150,000 and 200,000 people show up in a town of 25,000 is a monumental task that requires dozens of chairpersons, hundreds of volunteers and the complete cooperation of the City of Troy.

Much like the famous Macy's Thanksgiving Day Parade, when one festival ends, the planning for the next one begins almost immediately.

"June is tying up all the loose ends from that current festival," said Roetter, the current festival manager. "The nonprofits have that whole month to settle up with us on the donation they make back to us for letting them have a booth at the festival. And then we always have a sit-down meeting to evaluate how things went with the City of Troy and to figure out what we are going to do for the next year. And then typically, the first loose meeting of the festival committee happens sometime in early July."

By the time that meeting rolls around, the festival chairperson already has been in place for at least two years. The chairperson is a volunteer from the

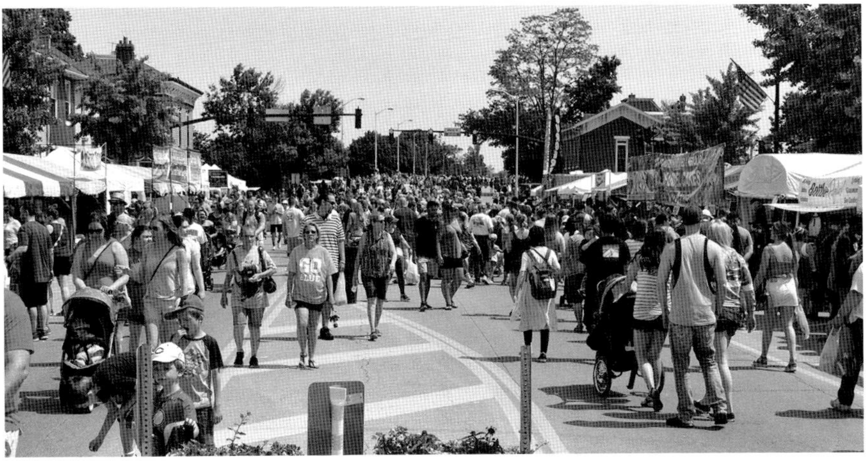

A crowd packs downtown Troy for the festival. *Courtesy of the* Troy Daily News.

community who serves for one year, while the festival manager is a full-time position. The festival manager also serves as the Troy Chamber of Commerce executive director. The festival chairperson is always selected from a group of people who have been in charge of major festival subcommittees.

"Typically, there's guidelines that they have to have been the chairperson of one of our bigger subcommittees, like publicity, transportation, arts and crafts, clubs and orgs or entertainment," Roetter said. "I think those are the five. So big. We want someone who has really seen the bigger aspects of how the festival works behind the scenes. It's important that [it's] someone that's been on site for the weekend and has seen the logistics behind the scenes."

Generally, the committee that selects the chairperson keeps it a secret from the honoree. "It's a surprise," Roetter said. "The announcements have been done differently over the years. So it usually involves a past chairperson, or as many as we can get, to go and surprise the person. It's more fun the more people you have. Mine was a little different because we had a chairman that resigned, so everybody got kind of moved up. And so sometimes we've gone to a restaurant. We usually have to convince that person that we are all just going out to dinner. And then the next thing you know, we start talking about the Strawberry Festival, and then you ask the question. I know I got to ask Nathan Walters, who followed me. We were at Mojo's [Bar and Grill], and his wife knew, so she was in on the surprise. And I just sort of slipped in a casual, 'What would you think about being in charge of 2015?' It almost went over his head because typically it's more of just a casual conversation.

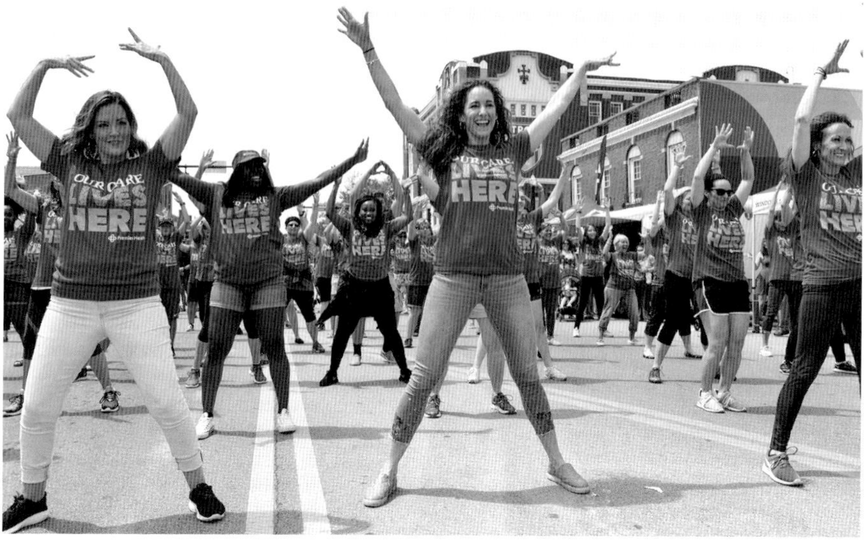

A flash mob breaks out at the Strawberry Festival. *Courtesy of the* Troy Daily News.

"And then I know that for Matt Watkins, we did it at Buffalo Wild Wings, and all the past chairmen hung out in the bar and then came over and celebrated with him."

Once the chairperson is selected, he or she has two years to continue volunteering with the festival, while at the same time continuing to learn from current and former chairpersons. During that time, the festival chairperson will select the theme for his or her festival.

Every festival since 1980—the first three festivals did not have themes—has had a theme. In the early days of the festival, the theme coincided with the parade, as floats and other units generally tried to incorporate the theme in some way. That combination between the theme and parade would eventually go by the wayside, but the theme would remain tied to each festival.

Typically, the chairperson picks a theme that has some sort of significance in their lives. The November before the festival, the chairperson announces it at a huge Strawberry Festival kickoff party.

"It usually happens right before Thanksgiving," Roetter said. "It's really exciting. People are just waiting to find out what the theme is going to be to find out if they're right. Because usually, the chairman tries to put their own spin on it and do things that are important for them, but still reflect the community. And so it's always interesting, people have this idea, like it's going to be this kind of thing…then they have to wait and see if they were right or not."

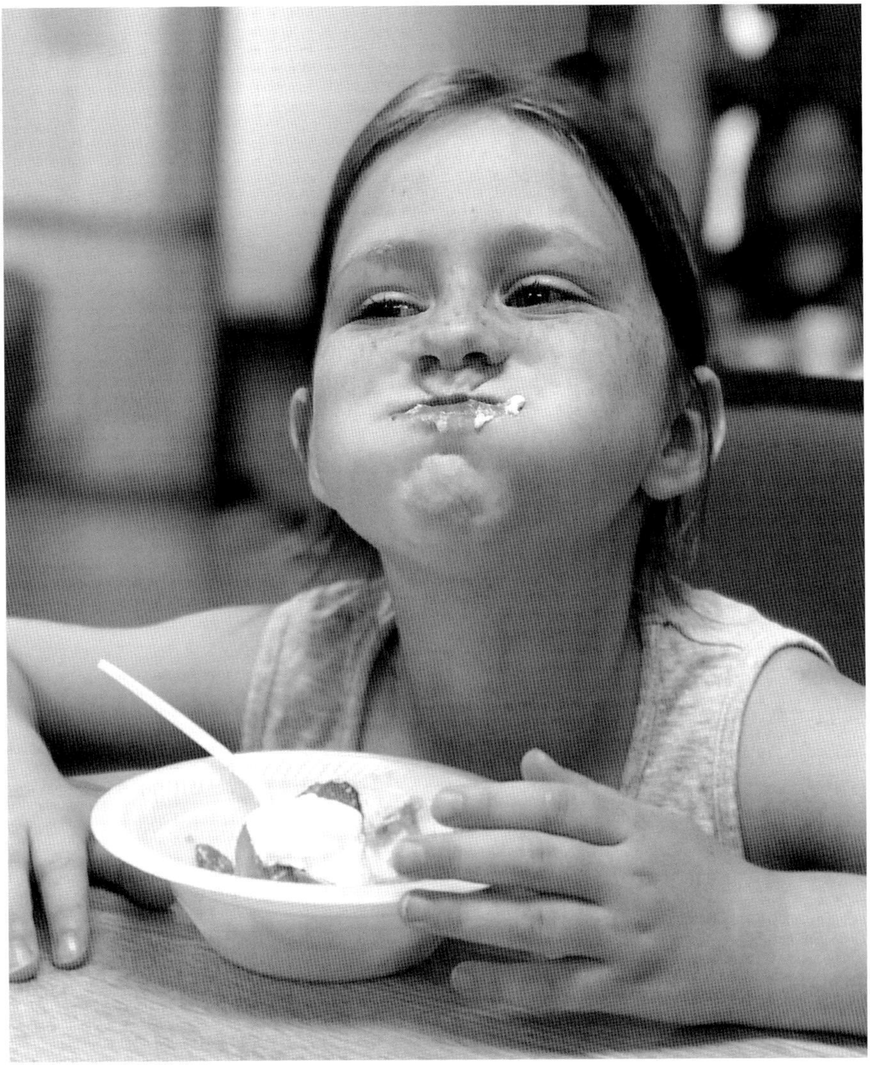

A young girl enjoys a bite of strawberry shortcake. *Courtesy of the Garrity family.*

That chairman and festival manager Roetter are then responsible for filling the roles of subcommittee chairpersons, each in charge of his or her own event. Many of those subcommittees are filled with the same volunteers year after year.

"The volunteers are truly the heart and soul of this festival," Roetter said. "Without the volunteers, there would be no Troy Strawberry Festival. They are really the ones who make it happen."

Roetter did admit, however, that it's becoming harder and harder to find volunteers, and many who currently are serving in volunteer roles have been doing so for quite some time. There are fewer new volunteers joining every year, which means the festival has had to look at the possibility of changing some things around to continue to make the festival run smoothly with its largely volunteer workforce.

"We have played around with the idea of having somebody take on more of the children's events because those are usually one-off events," she said. "And so, having someone do the big wheel race and the kids crawl instead of having multiple. We've never gotten there, and I think we can definitely combine if we were hurting for volunteers, but it's nice to have lots of hands on deck, and it helps us to build a leadership team so that we do have a nice pool of volunteers to choose from when it's time to pick a general chairman."

One thing that has never been lacking in the forty-plus-year history of the festival has been the support of Troy's city government. From the very first festival in 1977, the city has partnered with the festival, providing such services as water, electricity, sanitation, set-up and breakdown crews, as well as police officers, firefighters and emergency medical personnel.

"It does not happen without the city," Roetter said. "We could not do this for a number of reasons. I mean, they handle a lot of the behind-the-scenes

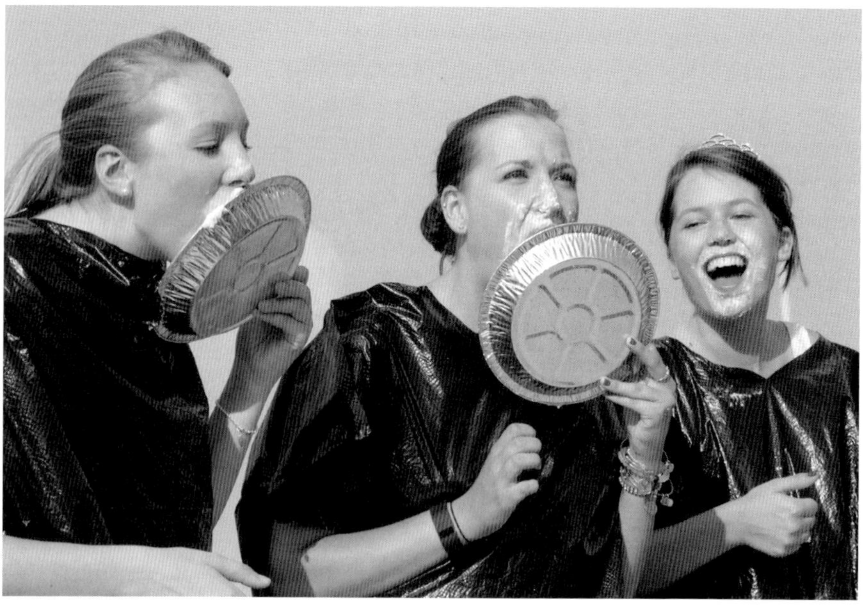

A group enjoys the aftermath of the pie-eating contest. *Courtesy of the* Troy Daily News.

logistics. Yeah, they come in ahead of time and help set up. I shouldn't even say 'help.' They do it all. They set up the barriers. They do all the heavy work. They set up and take care of all the water, all the electricity. The police, the firefighters, the paramedics. They're all on site with us that whole weekend. So it's not just the work that they're doing, it's also from the financial standpoint. I mean, if we had to contract those services out, we could not afford to have this festival.

"They have an in-kind donation. They give us in-kind services up to an amount. And then they charge us for services over and beyond that. It's a pretty generous donation."

The meetings among committee members start out monthly in July and then increase in frequency throughout the year. In the weeks leading up to the festival, the official meetings among committee members continue to increase.

By the time the week of the festival arrives, Roetter said, everyone is called into action for the final push before the start of the festival kickoff on that Friday.

"I would say, for this office and this city, that final week is really busy because we have to go out and mark the booth spaces on the streets and on the levee," Roetter said. "And loading starts on Wednesday night. That's bringing the food vendors in. So if they have a trailer, they load in on Wednesday night and get set before the tents go up on Thursday. And that happens, for the most part, Thursday throughout the day, as well as Wednesday evening.

"And then Friday, really—7:00 a.m., maybe 6:30 a.m. until 9:00 p.m., 9:30 p.m.—it is set-up all day long, answering questions, getting people in the right positions, working with the city to make sure that people's electricity is working. So it's just really busy. And probably two weeks out, the general chairman is busy because that is media week, so going out and talking to all the TV stations, radio, making sure everybody knows what's going on with the festival and if there's been any changes."

When the day of the festival somehow, someway, magically arrives, Roetter said she encourages the festival chairperson to enjoy himself or herself and to let the rest of the volunteers who are in place handle the smaller details.

"I can be crazy," Roetter said. "So we encourage the general chair that everything that they put in place is in place and enjoy the weekend and not be involved in putting out fires and troubleshooting. You let them go around and make appearances. And then the vice-chair or the next year's general chair and staff, we go around and put out fires and work with the city. Yeah, I'm doing that all weekend."

Roetter said the average festivalgoers only see the beautiful baby that is the festival at the very end—and don't have to concern themselves with the labor pains. Until you've volunteered for the festival and spent an entire weekend at the festival, it's hard to comprehend how much work goes into it, she said.

"It is insane," she said. "Yeah, for the general chair, it's a lot. And again, we talked about that. We're asking a chairman two to three years out. So they sit on the board of directors that oversees policy and procedures for the organization. And then there are also committee chairs on the Strawberry Festival Committee. So they are meeting, for the most part, about an hour a month leading up to January of the year.

"And then depending on their committee, they could be doing anywhere from two to five hours of volunteer work for the Strawberry Festival. And then that weekend, we really should just have some campers. Because that weekend, most of the core committee is onsite from start to finish. And while the festival ends at six o'clock on Sunday, we are usually here until sometime between nine and ten. And then at the end, they needed a partnership with the city. They are here overnight finishing everything and have everything taken down. If you drive through downtown Troy at 7:00 a.m. that Monday, you wouldn't even know there's been a festival here. The city is amazing."

After a year of planning, Roetter said, more often than not the festival itself goes by in a blink. And then, finally, there is time to relax when it is over.

"You're excited and we do a handoff at six o'clock when the festival ends," she said. "So you're excited to be able to celebrate the next year and just excited that everything came together. But yeah, by the time nine, ten o'clock rolls around, you're just so glad that it's over. So glad that it's over. Go home, put your feet up. Just a little bit."

Until it's time to start planning the next year's festival.

Chapter 19

THE FUTURE OF THE STRAWBERRY FESTIVAL

Every year, the fields at Fulton Farms are filled with strawberries. Some years they are bumper crops, and some years the juicy red fruits never quite reach their peak. But each year they are picked and consumed, knowing they will grow again the next season.

Such is the case with the Troy Strawberry Festival. Since 1977, the very first year of its existence, the Troy Strawberry Festival has come back again each subsequent year. Sometimes it was bigger and better than the year before. Sometimes it may not have lived up to the year prior. Much like its namesake fruit, some years it was entirely dependent on the weather. No matter what has happened, though, the festival never stopped growing along with the passing seasons.

Except, of course, when it ground to a halt.

In 2020, the COVID-19 virus swept around the globe, shutting down events and institutions that had been in place for decades. The Troy Strawberry Festival was not immune. For the first year since it began in June 1977, there was no festival. Having no festival had a devastating impact on the budgets for many nonprofits and local businesses and organizations that have come to depend on the festival as their main source of income.

"There are so many organizations that depend on the festival," Troy Chamber of Commerce executive director and Troy Strawberry Festival manager Kathi Roetter said. "For some of them, it's the only fundraiser they do. It's all they need to do. We are talking about a lot of money. I mean, a lot of money."

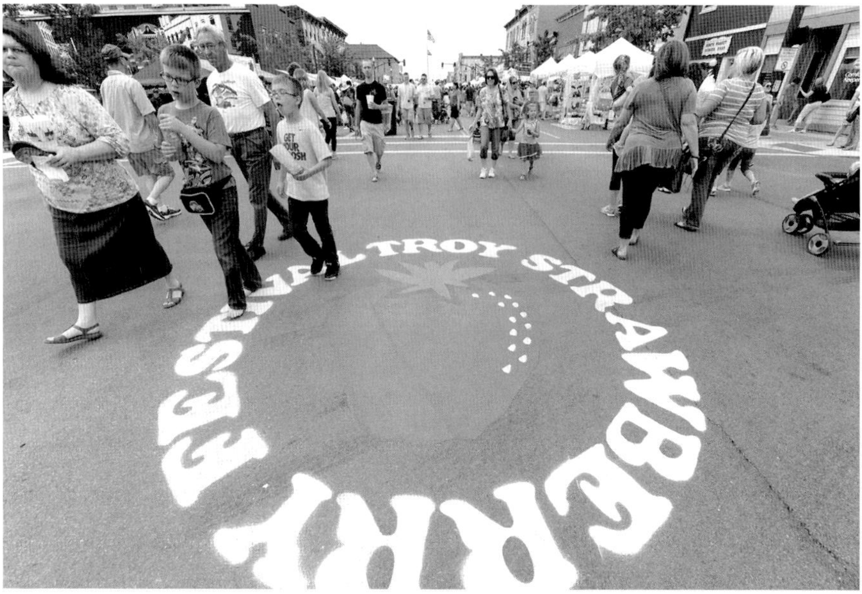

A large crowd passes over the Troy Strawberry Festival logo. *Courtesy of the* Troy Daily News.

As much as the money lost, however, at a time when people were struggling to find the positives in a world filled with fear and discord, Roetter knew taking away the festival tore a hole in the heart of the Troy community.

"That's what hurt the most, knowing how much it means to the people of Troy," Roetter said. "This is something people are proud of. This is a part of Troy. When you think of Troy, a lot of people think immediately of the Strawberry Festival. We knew when we made the decision to shut it down, it would be affecting the lives of so many people."

Ultimately, however, Roetter and the Troy Strawberry Festival Board of Directors knew it was the right decision. On March 13, Ohio governor Mike DeWine announced a two-week shutdown of schools, government agencies and nonessential businesses. He would continue to extend those deadlines throughout the rest of the spring.

On April 3, the Troy Strawberry Festival announced it would officially be canceling the festival for that year.

Roetter said the decision to cancel the festival so early—a move that would turn out to be the right decision, as the governor's office ultimately continued to shut down large gatherings of people throughout the summer of 2020—was made in part to protect the festival's vendors and nonprofit clubs and organizations.

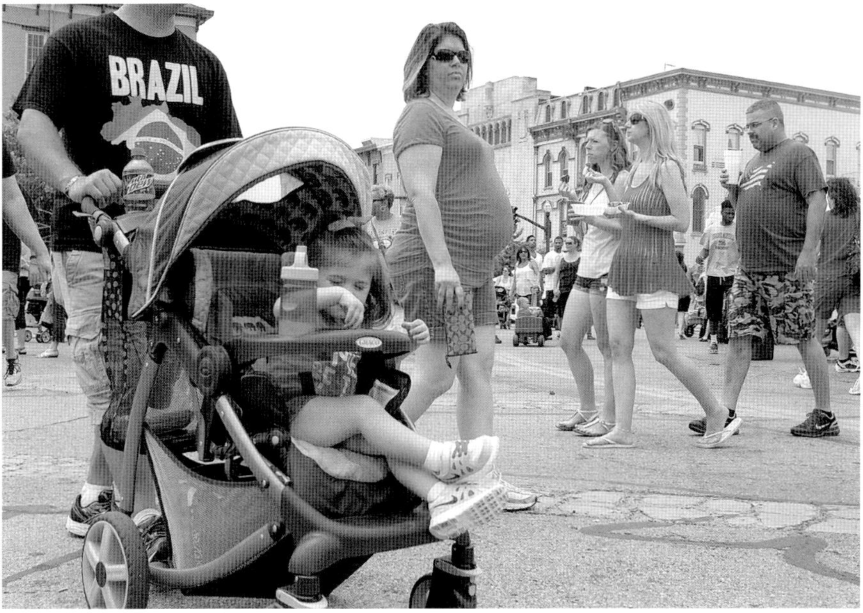

A man pushes a child in a stroller during the Strawberry Festival. *Courtesy of the* Troy Daily News.

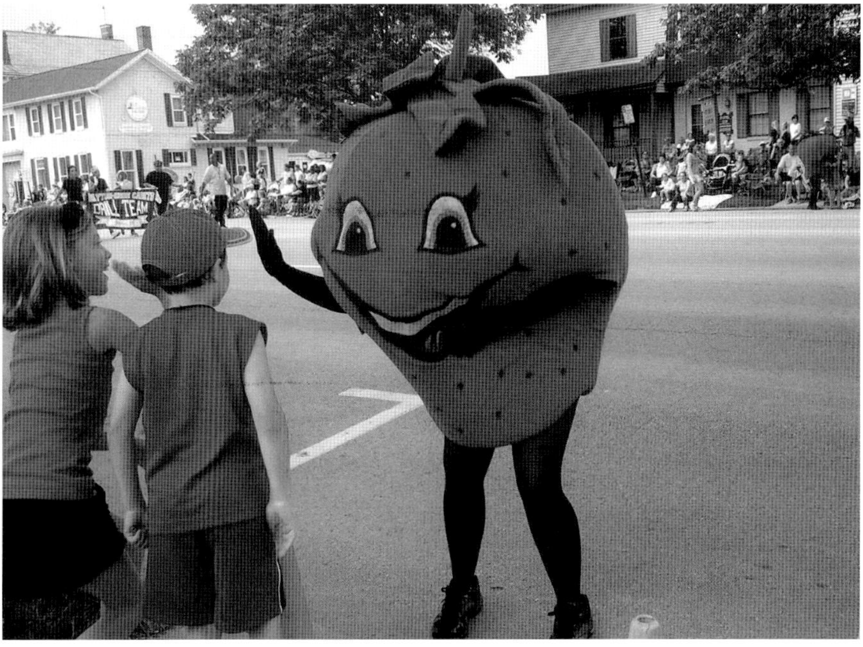

The Strawberry mascot high-fives a paradegoer. *Courtesy of Eric Brogan.*

"So we actually in March put out a call and told everyone, 'Let's hold tight. Let's see what this looks like. Don't send money at this point in time. Everybody's on hold,'" Roetter said. "And we probably updated our vendors maybe about every three weeks because the board continued to talk about it. And then once we were under the stay-at-home order, I mean, we knew at that point in time. There was just no way that we were going to have a festival with 150,000 people.

"It was a really big decision. But I would say that the board members that we have right now, they all knew that that was the decision that had to be made. I mean, there really was no conflict in making the decision. We knew it was going to be an emotional decision for the community. We have several nonprofits that have reached out to us because they were in the process of purchasing in March. So we canceled in April, and people just didn't understand why. They're like, 'Why wouldn't you wait?' Well, because we didn't want to spend any more money and we didn't want our nonprofits spending any more money. That was really what it was about. We could not put our nonprofits in a position where we move forward with the festival and then had to cancel it a week out or two weeks out. It just was not an option."

Roetter said after the cancellation of the 2020 Troy Strawberry Festival, as everyone began to learn more about masks, social distancing and other health and safety measures, the decision was made to hold a 2021 Troy Strawberry Festival, even if it meant holding a scaled-down or modified version of what had been held in previous years.

The Troy Strawberry Festival had to go on.

"We're planning on moving ahead, and we have vendors that have been to other festivals that still happen that have been calling and been giving us tips on what to do and who to talk to," Roetter said. "We've talked about the social distancing and maybe not providing some of the things like the [shuttle] busing, don't provide the transportation, let people figure it out on their own. That's not something we would prefer to do, but it may be something we have to do to ensure we can have a festival.

"The festival means a lot to the people of Troy. We caught a lot of flak from not having this year's festival. So, I mean, it's just really important because it's a tradition. And I think that if you would have to cancel two years in a row, it just, you lose the consistency and then the momentum with the organization and the giving for the nonprofits, too.

"I feel like we have to have it. I feel like we have to for that momentum and for the community. But I just feel like, for the organization, we have to because financially, we cannot go without a festival for two years. It was a hard enough hit this year."

Eventually, Roetter knows there will come a day when things will return to normal and she won't have to worry about planning a festival in the midst of a global pandemic. So not only does she have a plan for 2021 but for years down the road, as well. She not only wants the festival to come back as strong as it once was but to continue to grow into the future for generations yet to come.

"Being able to adapt is really important," Roetter said. "I mean, that's one of the things that you just have to do. That's why we made some of the big changes we did from 2012 to 2014. We looked at other festivals, like the Heritage Festival in Piqua and another big festival in Dayton. They were all starting to struggle. And so it's important that we are always looking at the financial side of it, but also, what does this look like from volunteer time? Because every organization out there, it struggles for volunteers anymore. What is cool and trendy? What do people want? What kind of experiences do they want today versus what we were when we were really this hometown festival with all these other events? That's not what people who are coming to the festival are looking for.

"We talk a lot about that just as generations are changing, we have to be willing to change. Because today, younger people want experiences. We're really trying to figure out what does that experience look like; what does the festival look like five years from now, ten years from now?"

Roetter said she and the rest of the festival planners have some ideas in mind. "Well, I would say continued focus on the entertainment," she said. "That is something that we started a couple years ago, and really putting our money into booking entertainers from around the area to help draw crowds. So really quality entertainment so that people wanted to bring chairs and stay and really sit and listen. And I would say that knowing the direction that people are going and that people want experiences, we would really love to be able to offer a beer garden and offer a Strawberry Festival beer, hopefully, with a local brewery. Because we just want to continue to make it about experiences.

"And then one of our other goals is to really make it a destination festival. We feel like it already is. I mean, we're one of the largest festivals in Ohio. But with that, how can we improve it and really connect it a little bit more to the community?"

For more than four decades, the Troy Strawberry Festival has grown like a strawberry on a bush. It has meant so much to so many in a small community. It is a point of pride and used to mark the start of summer.

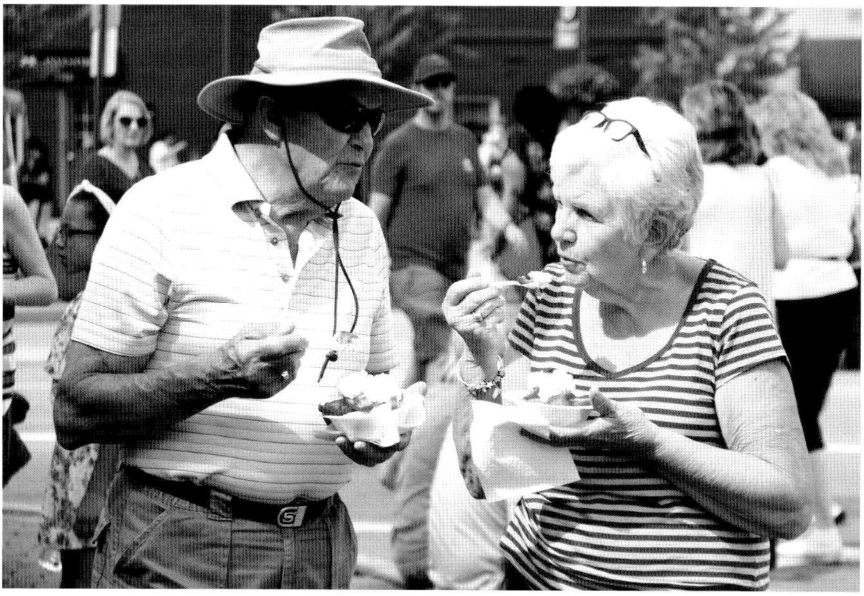

A couple shares a strawberry treat. *Courtesy of the* Troy Daily News.

It's more than a festival named after a sweet red fruit. It's a festival that was born out of a desire to help others. For four decades, it has been a festival that shone a spotlight on a small town that isn't afraid to dream big. It's been a source of memories for thousands. It's bigger than any one person or event.

The Strawberry Festival is everything that is good about Troy.

Appendix

STRAWBERRY FESTIVAL LISTS

Strawberry Festival Themes

There was no official Troy Strawberry Festival theme from 1977 to 1979.

1980: A Family Affair
1981: As American As…
1982: Kids Are the Berries
1983: The World According to Strawberries
1984: Go for the Berries
1985: Volunteers Are the Berries
1986: A Decade of Strawberry Magic
1987: A Picnic of Strawberries
1988: The Time Is Ripe
1989: Hats Off to the Strawberries
1990: The Great Strawberry Shake
1991: Straw'bear'y Delight
1992: Taste of Strawberry Country
1993: Strawberry Fields Forever
1994: Pig Out on Strawberries
1995: Race for the Berries
1996: Berried Treasure
1997: Berry Christmas
1998: It's a Berry Big World
1999: Remembering Berry Days
2000: Troy, The Berry Heart of It All
2001: 25 Berry Good Years
2002: All Abuzzzz…About Strawberries
2003: Spotlight on Strawberries
2004: Heavenly Strawberries
2005: Cruisin' the Berry '60s
2006: All-American Berries 30 Years
2007: Strawberryville
2008: Let's Talk Berries
2009: Dance to the Music
2010: Volunteers, Changing the World
2011: Berry Thankful Hearts
2012: Mardi Gras Berries
2013: A Magical Place
2014: Homegrown Berries
2015: Bowling for Berries
2016: A Capella Berries

2017: Silver Screen Berries
2018: Berrypalooza
2019: A Berry WACO Weekend

Strawberry Festival Chairperson

1977: Steve Hamilton
1978: Doug Trostle
1979: Rick Jackson
1980: Tom Thokey
1981: Charlene Walther
1982: Max Stubbs
1983: Malvern Timm
1984: Earl Burley
1985: Steve Kalmar
1986: Tim Lanahan
1987: Jan Manning
1988: Mike Beamish
1989: Tim Fourman
1990: Dan Plow
1991: Dee Morton (Mahan)
1992: Rick Riechert
1993: Jim Hall
1994: Joe Mahan
1995: Bill Myers
1996: Diana Thompson
1997: Chuck Lobaugh
1998: Tom Kendall
1999: Jody Davis
2000: Stan Kegley
2001: Phil Trentine
2002: Sally Riechert
2003: Roberta Jacobs
2004: Susan Fogt
2005: Steve Emmel
2006: John Schweser
2007: Tom Cooney
2008: Fred Daffner
2009: Becky Pappas
2010: Dave Pappas
2011: David Geiger
2012: Corie Schweser
2013: Jon Dankworth
2014: Kathi Roetter
2015: Doug Stone
2016: Nathan Walters
2017: Matt Watkins
2018: Eric Roetter
2019: Bruce Adamson

Strawberry Festival Parade Chairpersons

There was no Troy Strawberry Festival Parade from 1977 to 1979. The parade was discontinued following the 2014 Strawberry Festival when the festival made a permanent move to downtown Troy, through which the parade had run in all previous festivals.

1980: Earl Burley
1981: Earl Burley
1982: Susan Jackson
1983: Tim Lanahan
1984: Tim Lanahan
1985: Dave and Kim Wortman

1986: Rob and Jeanne Black
1987: Mike and Gail Merlo
1988: Mike and Gail Merlo
1989: Tom and Bev Kendall
1990: Jim and Naomi Hall
1991: Jim and Naomi Hall
1992: Mike and Kay McKelvey
1993: Mike and Kay McKelvey
1994: Mike McKelvey
1995: Jody Davis
1996: Jody Davis
1997: Jody Davis
1998: Charlie Olson
1999: Doug Black
2000: Doug Black
2001: Tom Cooney
2002: Tom Cooney and Jody Davis
2003: Jody Davis
2004: Jody Davis
2005: Jody Davis
2006: Matt Watkins
2007: Jody Davis
2008: Tom Cooney
2009: Tom Cooney
2010: Doug Stone
2011: Doug Stone
2012: no parade
2013: Doug Stone
2014: Matt Watkins

Parade Grand Marshal

1980: Steve Hamilton
1981: Troy All-American football players Bob Ferguson, Tom Vaughn and Tom Myers
1982: essay winners (nine students)
1983: Bob Cramlet
1984: John Slonaker
1985: William Hobart
1986: Earl Good
1987: Charles Hormel Jr.
1988: Frank E. Bazler
1989: Troy Foundation Board
1990: O.S. (Jack) Metcalf
1991: the Fulton family
1992: Paul and Doris Klein
1993: Mr. and Mrs. Ralph Yaggi
1994: John and Joseph Patten (twins)
1995: Rex and Jan Bigelow
1996: Bob and Jane Russell
1997: Stanley J. Phillips
1998: Donald Meek
1999: Reverend Ed Sensenbrenner
2000: Richard Klockner
2001: Mary Catherine Rozelle
2002: Miami County World War II veterans
2003: Mayor Peter E. Jenkins
2004: Ruben Pelayo
2005: Miami County Vietnam veterans
2006: Arthur "Ozzie" Haddad
2007: Dr. Mark Hess
2008: William Lohrer
2009: Thom and Pat Robinson
2010: Miami County Korean War veterans
2011: Operation Cloverleaf
2012: no parade
2013: Bob and Ann Baird
2014: Stewart and Marilyn Lipp

Troy Strawberry Festival Queen

1977: Patricia Ording
1978: Tina Erickson
1979: Laura Fleming
1980: Debbie Fuller
1981: Mary Hemmert
1982: Darci Delcamp
1983: Tanya Bailey
1984: Rhonda Swallow
1985: Kelly Miller
1986: Tamara Biser
1987: Jackie Huelskamp
1988: Valerie Davis
1989: Amy Beres
1990: Nicole Burton
1991: Kari Beres
1992: Kimberlee Eichhorn
1993: Heather Mitchell
1994: Hailey Waters
1995: Stacy Larson
1996: Emily Poling
1997: Crystal Berry
1998: LaTisha Martin
1999: Kristen Swinehart
2000: Jennie Middleton
2001: Avery McKinney
2002: Lindsay Easton
2003: Danielle Jay
2004: Tiffany Carnes
2005: Abigail Hardman
2006: Karissa Conner
2007: Cathy Rawers
2008: Ginny Vehorn
2009: Shannon Phillips
2010: Taylor Martin
2011: Emily Henry
2012: Logan Rathman
2013: Rachel Zelnick
2014: Halee Mollette
2015: Bobbi Jo Myers
2016: Jasmine Gill
2017: Sierra Simon
2018: Brooke Klopfenstein
2019: Abby Johnson

Miss Junior Strawberry

This event was only held from 2003 to 2012.

2003: Brooke Field
2004: Jade Green
2005: Hillary Budd
2006: Molly Jarvis
2007: Brooke Guillozet
2008: Shai Emerick
2009: Brenna Abbot
2010: Hannah Stickel
2011: Tabitha Sexton
2012: Maria Blocher

Little Miss Strawberry

1977: Alisa Musser
1978: Stephanie Hammer
1979: Karla Bartel
1980: Stacy Chaney
1981: Julie Allen
1982: Darci Puryear
1983: Jennifer Stephens
1984: Angela Overbay
1985: Jenny Taylor
1986: Abby Gayle Johnson
1987: Misty Miller
1988: Stephanie Dawn Deal
1989: Lacey Adams
1990: Brittania Buirley
1991: Katy Warner
1992: Lindsey Warner
1993: Kelly Hergenrather
1994: Jacquelyn Kerns
1995: Ashley James
1996: Amanda Werling
1997: Kalesha Rene Morris
1998: Taylor James
1999: Brooke Guilozet
2000: Jessica Williams
2001: Morgan Harder
2002: Hayley Nicole Ryan
2003: Bailey Dornbusch
2004: Eden Harbour
2005: Kayla Workman
2006: Skyler Nallen
2007: Katie Robinson
2008: Victoria Glover
2009: Jovie Studebaker
2010: Kaylee Tillman
2011: Whitney Welch
2012: Isabel Eichhorn
2013: Willow Isabella Miller
2014: Jayla Leeland
2015: Scarlett Williamson
2016: Elizabeth Sowers
2017: Eleanor Anderson
2018: Emily Verrill
2019: Adelynn Poeppelman

Little Mister Strawberry

1977: Gary Teach Jr.
1978: Brian Peoples
1979: Eric Grenert
1980: Mark Walburg
1981: Christopher Ziemka
1982: Spencer Hamilton
1983: Andy Klepinger
1984: Brett Bashore
1985: Brad Trostle
1986: Zane Shuman
1987: Nicholas Johnston
1988: Rusty Allen Gass
1989: Jake Strachan
1990: Nathaniel Deal
1991: Michael Allen Parminter
1992: Joshua Mahan
1993: Alan Marion
1994: Kristopher Hergenrather
1995: Joshua Deal
1996: Benjamin Rutter
1997: Jensen Lee Stidham
1998: Brandon Honeyman

1999: Zachary Roetter
2000: Kelton Webb
2001: Cody Niswonger
2002: Caleb Marlin
2003: Nicholas Neumier
2004: Montana Houshel
2005: Jackson Lee Davis
2006: Eli Sabins
2007: R.J. Bertini
2008: Nathan Rocke
2009: Henry Johnston
2010: Cooper Webb
2011: P.J. Glover
2012: Evan Couch
2013: Connor Haywood
2014: Matthew Waller
2015: Devon Miller
2016: Liam Edwards
2017: Owen Popplemen
2018: Trace Chaney
2019: Hudson Apple

Troy Strawberry Festival Golden Couple

The Troy Strawberry Festival Golden Couple competition began in 1999.

1999: Dick and Ruth Falter
2000: Bill and Mary Ann Cusac
2001: Richard and Janet Knife
2002: Roger and Nancy Kirk
2003: Arlen and Clara Reed
2004: Harold and Jean Melvin
2005: Melvin and Wanda Hackett
2006: Richard and Eugenie Markley
2007: Robert and Janet Laughman
2008: Harold and Jean Melvin
2009: Ray and Lillian Holmes
2010: Ralph and Lorraine Craig
2011: Ted and Dot Ristoff
2012: Shirley and Jake Heffner
2013: Bill and Connie Miller
2014: Bill and Carla Lohrer
2015: Sheila and Homer Baldwin
2016: Earl and Carol Burley
2017: Linda and Carl Sexauer
2018: Linda and Carl Sexauer
2019: no event

Troy Strawberry Festival Featured Entertainer

Not every Troy Strawberry Festival has had a featured entertainer.

1978: RIVER I
1979: RIVER II
1980: Air Force Band
1981: Miami County All-Star Band
1982: Miami County All-Star Band
1983: McClain Family Band
1985: McGuffy Lane
1987: DeGarmo and Key
1989: Hot Pursuit
1990: Sh-Boom

1991: Be-Bops
1992: Air Force Band of Flight
1994: B #Sharp
1995: Air Force Band of Flight
1996: The Dinosaurs
1997: M.C. Potts and Kevin Sharp
1998: The Turtles and Paul Revere and the Raiders
1999: The Kentucky Headhunters
2000: BTO
2001: Kim Fox
2002: Air Force Band of Flight
2003: McGuffy Lane
2004: Mike Albert as "Elvis"
2005: Backbeat (Beatles tribute)
2006: Tequilla Sunrise (Eagles tribute)
2007: Parrots of the Caribbean (Jimmy Buffett tribute)
2008: The Vogues
2009: Zoso (Led Zeppelin tribute)
2010: Gas Pump Jockeys
2011: Robyn Lacy and DeZydeco
2012: Bruce in the USA
2013: McGuffy Lane
2014: Red Hot Rhythm Review
2015: Gas Pump Jockeys
2016: Fourth Avenue
2017: Exploit

ABOUT THE AUTHOR

David Fong is a lifelong Troy, Ohio resident who has attended dozens of Troy Strawberry Festivals over the years. He is a 1992 graduate of Troy High School and a 1996 graduate of The Ohio State University, where he majored in journalism. After twenty-two years working at the *Troy Daily News*, he began working for the Troy City Schools in 2019 as director of communications. He also is the author of The History Press's *Ohio's Troy vs. Piqua Football Rivalry: The Battle on the Miami*. He lives in Troy with his wife, Michelle; daughter, Sophie; son, Max; and feisty dog, Millie Jo.